Th

Well-balanced, biblically sound, and use...
A practical tool that avoids extremes to determine the possible status of abuse. Every biblically oriented counselor needs to have this book available. Anne provides direction to further additional dependable biblical resources to assist with addressing the issue of abuse.

Dr. Howard Eyrich,
Director of Biblical Counseling
D.Min Program,
Birmingham Theological Seminary, **USA**

Anne addresses one of the most overlooked sin issues in her book and uses her vast experience in discipleship and biblical counseling to minister to women broken by emotionally abusive marriages. The book is designed to provide biblical insights for women who are struggling in emotionally abusive relationships and for the churches that want to help them. It provides a practical approach to understanding and applying biblical theology by using descriptive case studies and reflective questions at the end of each chapter. I look forward to using this book with my counselees.

Shannon Kay McCoy,
MABC, ACBC,
Biblical Counseling Director,
Valley Center Community Church,
CA, USA;
Council Member of the *Biblical Counseling Coalition*;
and author of *Help! I'm A Slave to Food*

Emotional abuse can often seem to be a vague concept, but in her book Anne gives a clear definition and description. She also provides specific ways for the victim to understand what's happening and how to respond biblically. Anne also describes how the church can counsel and intervene in ways that are compassionate and helpful – both to the wife who is being abused and to the husband in a way that offers opportunity for repentance and change. A very helpful book for biblical counselors.

Don Roy,
D.Min Training Center Director, *Institute for Biblical*
Counseling and Discipleship,
Slidell, Louisiana, USA

Here is a resource that seeks to restore dignity to abused women through total immersion in relevant scriptural truths. 'The Emotionally Abusive Husband' is an easy and essential read for those wanting to walk alongside wives who have been abused. I love how Anne helps the reader see that courageously changing the way a woman thinks about and responds to the abuse of her husband provides a potential opportunity for his dignity and worth to also be restored. Whether or not he changes is between him and God, but it is also influenced by how church leaders engage both the victim and perpetrator of the abuse. Anne's approach is thoroughly biblical, sensitive, and practical.

Jane Kratz,
Pastoral Care Counsellor, *Kommetjie Christian*
Church, **Kommetjie, South Africa;**
Vice-Chairman of *Biblical Counselling Africa*

People present us with many challenging situations. All of which require a theological understanding and applying biblical wisdom. The unloving and ungodly interaction between husband and wife is no exception and I am thankful for Anne providing us with a much-needed resource for helping us navigate this especially challenging situation in a God-glorifying way.

Andrew D. Rogers, PhD. Executive Director,
Overseas Instruction in Counseling

Helping women in abusive situations is one of the responsibilities of the local church. As Christians, we need to be equipped to know how to help. It was helpful to read a female perspective on an issue where husbands, church leaders, and brothers in Christ, need to do so much more. This book is an excellent resource to think through the subject biblically so that we can be better informed and more fully equipped to offer God-honoring support.

Alasdair McPherson,
Bible teacher

The Emotionally Abusive Husband

Also by Anne Dryburgh

*(Un)ashamed: Christ's Transforming Hope
for Rape Victims*

The Emotionally Abusive Parent

*Coming soon:
The Emotionally Abusive Mindset*

ANNE DRYBURGH

The Emotionally Abusive Husband

Its Effects and How to Overcome Them in Christ

Illumine Press

United Kingdom

COPYRIGHT © Anne Dryburgh, 2022

The moral right of the author has been asserted.

Previously published as *Debilitated and Diminished: Help for Christian Women in Emotionally Abusive Marriages* by the same author.

A CIP catalogue record for this book is available from the British Library

ISBN: 978-1-7398719-9-4 (paperback)

ISBN: 978-1-7398719-4-9 (e-book)

This book is dedicated to Martin and Lydia Symons,
who for decades have humbly helped countless people
suffering because of abuse.

About Anne

ANNE DRYBURGH, PH.D., is a biblical counselor certified by the *Association of Certified Biblical Counselors* (ACBC), the *International Association of Biblical Counselors* (IABC), and *The Addiction Connection,* a collective of biblical counselors and ministries united for the purpose of training and equipping the Body of Christ in biblically helping addicts and their loved ones. She has been a missionary with *Echoes International* in Flemish-speaking Belgium since the 1990s and partners with a number of biblical counseling organizations. She is the author of *(Un)ashamed: Christ's Transforming Hope for Rape Victims;* and *The Emotionally Abusive Parent: Its Effects & How to Overcome Them in Christ.*

Contents

Foreword

THE EMOTIONALLY ABUSIVE Husband is a tremendous, short book that reveals the depravity of man in a marriage relationship that has gone bad, but gives the hope of the Gospel that Christ can save us from our sins and transform our lives! Recently, this book had been used mightily in my family's lives. Thank you, Dr Dryburgh, for another compelling work!

Johnny Touchet, pastor and missionary, and founder of Partner 10:15 ministries

Introduction

EMMA HAD GIVEN up. Depressed, listless, and lifeless, she lay on her bed all day every day. For years she had been insulted, ridiculed, controlled, and punished by her husband Frank. While treating her in this way, he appeared to be spiritual to the other members of the church. When Frank left her for another woman, she gave up and spent the rest of her life in bed. It doesn't need to be this way though.

Olivia is in her seventies. Her husband, Stephen, treats her the same way Frank treated Emma. Despite doing all she could to love and care for him, things have not improved. Stephen knows that he can treat his wife however he wants – he will always get his own way. Olivia wonders what is wrong with her and why her husband won't love her.

Frank and Stephen treat their wives in emotionally abusive ways. In this book you will also meet Debbie and Pete and hear about their journey from an abusive marriage to a more healthy one.

During the thirty years that I have been involved in discipleship and biblical counseling, my heart has been broken numerous times by hearing such stories.

The suffering of these women has caused me to take this issue seriously, believing that there must be answers in the Bible for them to trust the Lord in their situation. With my whole heart I was convinced that there must be better answers in Scripture than the two typical answers that have been given: submit or divorce.

In order to ensure that the research I conducted was at the highest possible level, I studied this issue as my PhD dissertation topic. Along with my experience in helping abused women, this short book stemming from that research is designed to provide biblical insights for women who are in emotionally abusive relationships and for the women who are helping to support them. Most men will never deal directly with women involved in such situations, but my hope is that the book will also provide some helpful insights for them as they work with women who do and as they think through the support which the local church should provide in these situations; it may also provide some wisdom regarding any men they suspect may be abusive to their wives.

In recent years the issue of abuse in marriage has gained international attention, especially physical violence and emotional abuse. While considerable work has been conducted by secular researchers, up until recently little work has been done in the Christian world. Since writing the first edition of this book, there have been a few books written by biblical counselors to try to offer help in this complex area. Often when the subject of abuse has been addressed, there has been a tendency to focus on physical abuse and its consequences. These effects can include hurt, rejection, fear, anger, forgiveness, and shame. However, these issues are not confined to physical abuse: they can stem from emotional abuse as well. It is common for well-intentioned counselors to advise women to submit to their husbands unless they are asked to sin or are being physically abused. This approach, however, does not address how submission in some non-sin areas can lead to wives being controlled and manipulated by their husbands in emotionally abusive relationships.

How this book can help you

This two-fold aim of this book is to provide a resource for women in emotionally abusive relationships, and for those helping them. It does not cover physical or sexual abuse in marriage and it assumes that the position of headship is one of authority. I take the view that in practice headship refers to a husband laying down his life for his wife, not laying down the law. As a result, like the response of the church to Christ's sacrifice, a wife is more likely to respond to a husband's lead when she sees his love and sacrifice for her.

In this new, second edition of the book *Debilitated and Diminished: Help for Women in Emotionally Abusive Marriages* questions have also been added at the end of the first three chapters. These are designed for the emotionally abused woman as she seeks to know the Lord and apply the principles suggested in the book. Those counselling such women will also find the questions helpful.

What this book is not

A word of caution is necessary. Abusive situations are gravely serious. While insights have been suggested in this book, it is not the *definitive* answer about how to help abused women. It touches on subjects that are tremendously complicated and where time is needed to address these areas in an in-depth manner to be able to effectively help people. Well-intentioned but unwise advice can cause suffering and damage lives. Wisdom and insight are required on a case-by-case basis. There are no standard cut-and-dried answers. As someone said, 'one size does not fit all.'

1. Emotional Abuse – What it is

HANNAH WAS THE courageous one. Deep down, she knew something was just not right about her marriage to David. Ever since her wedding she had accepted that she was to blame for their difficulties. Each time David blamed her, she decided she would love him even more, believing this would make him less angry and benefit their relationship. As a Christian wife, she consciously chose to be submissive to his decisions and wishes, yet things kept getting worse. David wanted her to stay in the house all day. She was not allowed any friends over to visit. Whenever she did something he perceived to be wrong, there would be a torrent of insults about how bad a wife she was. After adapting to his expectations, there would be another torrent of insults, this time demanding that she be who she was in the first place. For example, David would shout at her about how the furniture was arranged in the living room, only for him to shout at her again when she rearranged it to suit his wishes. Hannah was fearful, hurt, angry, and aware that she was heading toward depression.

A definition of emotional abuse

Does Hannah's story resonate with you? We know that conflict happens in every marriage, but the kind of constant conflict you may be experiencing in your marriage is different than one that is simply going through a time of difficulty. Verbally assaulting a spouse during an argument does not make the relationship abusive. Behavior that *is* emotionally abusive is when it exhibits a consistent pattern that is designed to control another person. The other person responds to the controlling behavior by becoming dependent upon the perpetrator.

When we are trying to understand the nature of emotional abuse, it is helpful to accurately describe and define things. By having a correct understanding we can work towards change. Having a definition of emotional abuse is crucial, otherwise we run the risk that we could say that someone is abusive when they are not. None of us would want to be guilty of wrongly accusing people.

A definition of emotional abuse is:

"Any non-physical behavior that is designed to control, intimidate, subjugate, punish, or isolate another person resulting in the victim becoming emotionally, behaviorally, and mentally dependent on the abuser."[1]

We can break this down further by looking at some of the behaviors typical of an abusive husband. Emotionally abusive husbands commonly use verbal abuse, coercion and threats, minimizing, denying and blaming, intimidation, playing mind games, isolation, male privilege, financial control, using the children, exhibiting two different personalities, jealousy, and good periods. These behaviors work together to lead him to having control over his wife. We will be looking at each of these in the next chapter.

> *Behavior that is emotionally abusive is when it exhibits a consistent pattern that is designed to control another person. The other person responds to the controlling behavior by becoming dependent upon the perpetrator.*

Wives react in certain ways too. Common responses are confusion, doubt, fear, guilt, worry, inhibition, anger, shame, a changed mental state, emotional, behavioral, and mental dependence upon the abuser, physical ailments, loneliness, depression, and sorrow.

Debbie's story

When Debbie married Pete, her dreams had been fulfilled. Pete was charming, caring, attentive, and attended the same church as she did. After dating during college, they moved town to where Pete had landed a job in new tech firm. He was well-liked because of his care for people. One of the things that attracted her to him at college was that he talked about all believers living as image-bearers and how important it is that women are not held back in any way from living the life that the Lord has for them. Debbie was convinced that she had married a godly man. And she wanted to be a godly helper, so did all she could to express her love for him. When Pete was upset, she made sure that she did everything possible to make him happy again. Yet whenever he was upset, it always seemed to be her fault. She would submit to him and try harder to love him and make him happy. No matter what she did, Pete would tell her how bad a wife she was. Debbie was always thinking about how Pete would treat her, what he would say to her, and how he would behave toward others. Instead of living to please God first, Debbie was now being controlled by Pete.

2. Emotional Abuse Expressed and Experienced

WHENEVER CHRIS WAS in the room, he was very present. Everyone could sense what mood he was in and that he expected his wife, Carla, to please him. It was awkward listening to the way that he joked about her. Although his comments were cloaked in humor, they were quite demeaning. He would shame and humiliate her in front of us and say how disgusted he was with her. As "the man of the house" he said he always got the most of everything and made all the decisions. He had an expensive car, a motorbike, and kept up to date with the latest gadgets. If he wanted anything, he bought it. Carla, in contrast, had no money of her own, had to stick rigidly to a food budget made by Chris, and had to ask permission to spend money on anything else. The answer was an inevitable 'No'.

As we saw in the previous chapter, emotionally abusive husbands demonstrate a consistent pattern of behavior to gain control over their wives. If a husband treats his wife poorly by failing to care for her or by speaking to her in a mean way, this does not necessarily mean that he is being emotionally abusive. Let me explain. If a husband repeatedly lashes out in anger by insulting his wife during conflicts, this does not necessarily mean he is being abusive. While the way of speaking is clearly wrong, for him to be abusive he would need to be engaging in patterns of behavior to gain control over her.

Below are some of the behaviors involved in emotional abuse that are used to gain control. This should help you identify if this is what you are experiencing. Please take your time as you are reading this, as it could be upsetting.

Types of emotional abuse

Verbal abuse

If your husband is being verbally abusive, he will speak to you in an attacking or hurtful manner, with the purpose of leading you to believe something that is not true, or he will say things to you that are not true. It involves overt and covert abuse.

Overt abuse is "openly demeaning" behavior that includes belittling, yelling, name-calling, criticizing, ordering around, sulking, accusing, ridiculing, insulting, trivializing, expressing disgust toward you, threatening, blaming, humiliating, shouting, and shaming.[2]

> *Emotionally abusive husbands demonstrate a consistent pattern of behavior in order to gain control over their wives.*

Covert abuse is subtle. You are aware that something is wrong but are not certain what the real problem is. It includes discounting (when someone treats you and your opinions as unreliable or unimportant), negating (contradicting or denying things you say), accusing, denying, labeling, using subtle threats, disapproving facial expressions, a sarcastic tone of voice, implying that you are inadequate, joking to diminish you, interrupting you, and twisting and distorting what you say.3

When he called you names, did he speak in ways that attacked your humanity, femininity, even lowering you to the status of an animal or a body part? At times he may have used technical language which he thought you wouldn't understand.

Coercion and threats

If your husband uses coercion, he will try to persuade or restrain you by force. Has your husband threatened you? He could have made threats about things you depend on such as food, money, clothing, medicine, and the children. Has he threatened to withdraw emotionally, ignore you, and even to commit suicide?

Has he tried to control you while trying to frighten you? Examples are leaving anonymous threats on your voicemail, removing clothing or memorabilia, slashing tires, and stealing mail. Has he used secrets that you have told him to his own advantage, or behaved in an embarrassing way in public? Since you do not know whether or not he will carry out his threats, have you come to live in a state of anxiety, despair, and helplessness? If you have, your husband could now be able to control every detail of your daily life: even to the extent of what you eat; when, where, and how you drive a car; how you dress; how you wash yourself; and what you watch on television or the Internet.

Minimizing, denying, and blaming

Does your husband habitually minimize you and attempt to invalidate your feelings and how you experience life? Minimizing includes trivializing and discounting what you think and do. He might also discount your achievements. An example would be saying that anyone can pass exams nowadays if you gain a qualification that he does not have.

Does he deny that the abuse has happened, what he is clearly feeling, or the truth or reality of what you think, what you feel, your perceptions, and even claim that he knows them better than you do?

Does he consistently blame you for *his* behavior? If he does, he is avoiding the things that are bothering him and the feelings that go along with them. By doing this he is making you responsible for what he does. By blaming you, he is able to prevent you from confronting him, and from considering his own actions.

You will be blamed because he believes that you exist to make him happy. If he is not happy, he believes that it is your fault. Using minimizing, denying, and blaming is an attempt to control your thinking so that it conforms to how he sees life.

Intimidation

If he uses intimidation, he may be trying to control circumstances or to cause you to live in fear or helplessness. When he is trying to intimidate you, he might get too close to you when he is angry, block your way, claim that his behavior is an attempt to make you listen, or drive the car aggressively as a way of trying to scare you. The three most common intimidating behaviors used are threats, surveillance, and degradation.[4] If you are living in a state of fear, you might give into his attempt to control you, even though you have not been physically hurt. If you have given in, you probably did this because you had imagined what could possibly happen to you.

Mind games

If your husband is emotionally abusing you, he will try to make you doubt your own thinking. If he succeeds in this, it will result in you becoming dependent on him. Various tricks are used, such as making remarks that cause confusion. Examples are "I am telling you this for your own good," "That never happened," and "You are just imagining it."[5] The subject of conversation may be overtly or covertly changed, he may be adamant that you are thinking things that you weren't, and twist what you say. At times he may be charming toward others, causing you to doubt whether someone who is so nice could be so bad. If he accuses you of having an evil character, it could lead you to becoming confused and doubting whether you can trust your own thinking and values.

This is the point when you will accept that his judgments about you are true.

"Gaslighting" is a commonly used term to explain this type of behavior. The term comes from a 1938 play called 'Gaslight' in which a husband tries to convince his wife that she is insane so that he can steal from her. The husband says and does things that leads his wife to doubt her own perceptions. For example, he may call you to ask you to pick something up for him, but later deny that he called. Or he may not call you and ask you why you did not do as he asked. Or he tells you that he likes his steak to be well-done after having told you that he always likes his steaks rare. Things might be taken from you for an unknown reason, only to reappear after you have looked for them for a long time. This could result in you thinking that you are losing your mind.

Isolation

If your husband is engaging in emotional abuse, he might isolate you by removing your support system of friends and family. He will probably believe that you should be there only for his needs and because other people might help you be more independent and stronger. Which he doesn't want. If he tries to isolate you, he could do this by complaining when you have contact with others, shaming or embarrassing you in front of others, stalking you, having you move house to a remote location, or forbidding you to leave the house. Once you have become isolated, he will be able to give you false information, which then cannot be corrected by others since they are not around. This leads to you becoming mentally dependent upon him.

Male privilege

In order for abuse to occur, there must be inequality in the relationship. If your husband is emotionally abusive, he will probably see you as his inferior regarding your gender, intelligence, and ability to use and understand logic. If he believes that proper masculinity involves a man controlling and dominating his wife, then he might control you, he may think that it is unfeminine of you to doubt or question his instructions. You could be expected to allow him to make decisions, while fulfilling your womanly role of cooking, cleaning, caring for the children, and catering to his every need.

Financial control

Does your husband not give you enough money to be able to pay for daily or weekly expenses? Does he deprive you of money to buy essentials while spending a lot on himself? If you had your own bank account before you married, he probably made you give it to him. If you are employed, he might make you give what you earn to him. The family assets may have been put in his name. He may have required a detailed account of everything that you spend, accompany you when you need to spend money, and require that you seek permission before you do. If he is displeased with you, he might remove your access to money, even if you have a legitimate claim to it.

Since you could not survive financially without him, this will lead you to being under his control.

Using the children

If you come to the realization that you could not survive financially on your own, you might continue to put up with the abuse so that you can care for your children. If your husband senses that he is losing power over you, he might begin to verbally abuse the children. Seeing them hurt will be distressing for you. He might demand too much from them and punish them when they fail, threaten them, or say that he will harm them.

Having two personalities

Is your husband well-liked by other people? Do outsiders think that he is an upstanding citizen? He might relate to people outside the home in a mature way. He may be calm with outsiders while being an angry man at home; be generous toward outsiders, but selfish at home; or promote women's rights with outsiders yet be derogatory about women when he's back home. Since others believe that he is a respected pillar of society you know that they will probably not believe you or may think that any trouble in your relationship is your fault. After all, he's such a nice guy: aren't you a fortunate woman!

Jealousy

Is your husband characterized by jealousy? Does he expect that you prove your love for him while being possessive of you? Does he demand that you give all your attention to him, or accuse you of being interested in other men when there is no reason to suspect this? His jealousy, possessiveness, and suspiciousness could lead to him stalking you by, for example, calling you several times a day, expecting you to spend all your free time with him, checking what you do with your time, and keeping track of your location via your cell phone's GPS system or other method. Any achievement you make will probably be seen as competition and as a threat to him.

Good periods

After a period of treating you badly he might begin to treat you well. After expressing regret about his bad behavior, there could be a period when he is kind, generous, and loving. This can lead you to hope that he is changing. If you do, you will probably start to invest in the relationship again. His new behavior reminds you of the person that you fell in love with. You will probably start to trust him and become vulnerable. In time, when he senses that he has "gotten away" with his bad behavior, and that you are emotionally vulnerable, it is likely that he will start to mistreat you again. This is because he believes that you belong to him and that he has regained control. These good periods are, however, part of his abusive behavior – they are not a change from it.

The effects of emotional abuse on you

These various behaviors will have a number of effects upon you. *Note:* You may not experience all of them, but those you do suffer from will be linked to each other.

Confusion

When your husband emotionally abuses you, you will probably become confused. If this happens, it is easier for him to manipulate you. Do you examine all that has happened to find something wrong with you that caused the abuse? Do you believe that knowing this will prevent it happening in the future? Are his behaviors too confusing for you to be able to see where you are wrong? For example, he might change the subject of the conversation or be adamant that you are thinking and feeling things which you are not. He might declare his love for you yet at the same time behave in a manner that expresses dislike for you. When he is with outsiders he might behave well, yet be abusive toward you behind the scenes. Does he later deny things that he has clearly said or done? If you accept what he says as true, you are inadvertently allowing him to interpret *your* experience of events. This will lead to you becoming even more confused.

Doubt

He will want you to doubt yourself. He does this by trying to get you to doubt your own perceptions and thinking ability. He might say things like, "You are just angry because you are not getting your own way, so you are saying that I am mistreating you."[6] He might say that you are illogical, being argumentative, being selfish, and/or always have to have your own way. He may state that your understanding of what is happening, and even your feelings, is misguided. Or, he could make a derogatory comment and then claim that he was only joking. If you believe him, you will come to doubt your own understanding and perceptions. This leads him to being able to control you.

Fear

Are you living in a state of fear? This happens because you wonder what he will be like when he comes home, when the abusive behavior will start again, going over in your mind what you should have said or done during previous abusive incidents, and trying to figure out how to make him understand you. If previous abusive incidents come to mind, you might become fearful or scared of saying or doing the wrong thing. This can lead you to being anxious when you are with him. You might watch his facial expressions, gestures, and tone of voice in order not to upset him. You could become fearful if he tracks your time, controls who you see and how much money you spend; decides how, when, and what you cook and what you can wear. If you speak to him about his behavior and he becomes angry, you will probably become fearful of his anger. If he threatens you, the children, or a family pet in some way, you will almost certainly live in fear. If you give in to fear, you could end up staying at home most of the time and becoming a recluse.

Guilt

He will probably try to make you feel guilty. He could go about doing this by coercing you to do something wrong, only to say afterwards that you are a bad person for having done it. Or he might claim that not going along with him is unfair to him, or that you are oppressing him by talking to him about the way he treats you. If you agree with him that you are the guilty one, you then become responsible for the success of the relationship.

Worry

You will probably start to worry. You may worry about what he will do to you, the children, what he says and does behind your back to others, and how he will treat you when he comes home. Even though it comes naturally to you to worry about how he will relate to you, this kind of thinking does not prevent or stop his abusive behavior.

Inhibition

Due to living in a state of fear of displeasing your husband and having lost trust in your own thinking and perception, you could become inhibited – lacking in confidence. This is especially true when he engages in stalking behavior, such as calling or texting you throughout the day, checking your emails and other messages, checking your location on his phone or other device, reacting angrily or sulking when you spend time with friends or family, or criticizing your clothing. When you are with other people, you could become concerned that you don't say or do something that will trigger an angry or sulky response from him. If you start responding in this way, you will become inhibited when you are with other people.

Anger

Are you angry at the way he treats you? Part of the reason for being angry could be because you are not able to change things. With time, your anger could grow into resentment. You might also be angry at yourself for giving in to his treatment and at other times for not doing anything about it. The anger that you experience could add to your guilt.

Shame

The shame that you experience is because you believe that you are bad. You probably think that there is something wrong with you and that you do not deserve to be accepted by others. You might feel shame because he does not love you, and for putting up with him humiliating you. The shame may lead you to become passive and helpless.

Changed mental state

The emotionally abusive behavior will affect your thinking. You might believe that you are inadequate, just as he claims. "Flooding" can occur, which is when flashbacks, intrusive thoughts, and/or painful memories bombard your thinking.[7] This will lead to your cognitive thinking and ability to judge being negatively affected. You could come to a point where you start to think that you are losing your mind. You will probably magnify his bad behavior and then minimize that bad behavior when he treats you better. Or you might magnify your faults and minimize your qualities.

You may come to believe that you are inadequate in some way. You could become easily distracted and preoccupied. You might find it difficult to concentrate and have a reduced capacity to perceive, think, and reason properly. This could lead you to doubt your judgment and/or perceptions. You could become obsessive about your situation, forgetful, lose things, become accident prone, and do things as an escape, such as overeating and oversleeping.

Emotional, behavioral, and mental dependence

It is likely that you will gradually become less communicative in order to avoid upsetting him. You might even stop saying what you think altogether, because you are scared of being called names by him. You may do this at first because you want to respect him, but you will eventually come to do this more often than not because you are scared of his anger. You may even think that there is something wrong with you for wanting to speak openly with him. He might demand that you do what he says in all areas of life. Examples are cooking, finances, clothing, housework, sexually, and the children.[8] You will eventually try to anticipate what he is thinking and wanting. You might believe that doing this can prevent him from becoming angry or that you will eventually be loved and accepted by him. If you come to the point of thinking that your thoughts and desires are unimportant, you will probably become dependent on his thoughts about you and behave accordingly. You could believe that you would not be able to survive if he left you. If there are times when he gives you the emotional connection that you crave, when he reverts back to being angry you may feel devastated and try to win back his love and approval.

Physical ailments

Since the mind and the body are interconnected, your thoughts in response to the abuse often affect your physical condition. It is claimed that victims of emotional abuse characteristically suffer from headaches, respiratory problems, arthritis, bladder problems, stomach problems, sleep disturbances, weight loss or gain, back pain, palpitations, or high blood pressure.[9]

Loneliness

Trying to keep his love and acceptance, only to be confronted with recurrent abuse, leads to loneliness. This comes from a lack of relationship with your husband or with other people who understand what's going on in your marriage. Your experience might be that you have no relationships with people who really understand you and your situation.

Depression

As well as feeling lonely in your isolated situation, you could become sad. This sadness can lead to depression. If you continue to put up with and give in to the abusive behavior, the more depressed you will become. If you live like this for a period of time, you could end of being in a constant state of depression.

Sorrow

If you internalize the abusive treatment, you will become sorrowful. Your sorrow is over the marriage that you had hoped for but never experienced, and for the husband who you wanted to love and appreciate. This husband appeared for brief moments but just as quickly disappeared.

Debbie's story

Debbie could see that Pete behaved in many of these ways toward her and that her responses were how victims typically respond. She decided that if she was to know the Lord and live in a God-honoring way in her situation, it would be essential for her to understand what the Bible teaches about her nature as a human being, the effect of sin on the marital relationship, how she is renewed in Christ, and what the Bible teaches about headship and submission.

Questions for Reflection

When answering the questions at the end of each chapter, please be as honest as you can before the Lord. As we live to glorify and honor the Lord, and examine our hearts in the process, we do not wish to shift blame or be unkind in any way. We need to take responsibility for our own actions without ignoring, minimizing or magnifying those of our partner. Our desire is to become the people God wants us to be.

1. When you relate to your spouse, what is uppermost in your thinking? Is it pleasing and honoring the Lord first and foremost?

2. As you seek to love your spouse, what are you longing for, what do you want in the relationship? Some examples are to keep the peace, to be accepted and loved, to reflect the Lord, and to love your spouse as the Lord calls you to.

3. Verbal abuse – are you and your spouse guilty of using demeaning words when you speak to each other? If so, in what way do you do this?

4. Coercion and threats – if you do what the Lord wants, does your husband insinuate that he will retaliate in some way? How does he do this? Does he behave in a way that frightens you? What does he do?

5. Minimizing, denying, and blaming – how does your husband respond to you when you give an opinion on something or share some of your experiences over the last few days? If your husband has treated you badly, what reason does he give for his behavior? On whom does he place the responsibility?

6. Intimidation – what types of behavior does he engage in which make you feel intimidated?

7. Mind games – does he respond to you by saying things such as "I never said that", "You are imagining it", or "That never happened"? Does he give contradictory instructions or express contradictory viewpoints?

8. Isolation – has your social circle decreased? What were the events that led up to this happening? What were you thinking about these people, yourself, and the response of your husband to them when you decided to withdraw from people?

9. Male privilege – what views of the nature of men and women do you and your husband hold? What are the views of each person's roles?

10. Finances – a whole range of views are held by godly couples about who should be responsible for the family finances. In your situation, are all the people in your family adequately provided for? Do you know what your financial situation is?

11. Children – how do you respond if he upsets or threatens your children (outside the bounds of agreed family discipline)? In what way are you tempted to neglect a godly approach of raising them when this happens?

12. Two personalities – does your husband behave in a different way when he is outside the home? How do you think people would respond if you were to tell them what he is *really* like?

13. Jealousy – does your husband make you prove your love for him? In what way? How does he treat you when you spend time with other people?

14. Good periods – when he treats you well, what hopes do you cherish? How do you change the way that you relate to him?

15. Confusion – when he is upset, do you examine yourself to see if you have contributed to the incident? This should lead you to seek to become more Christ-like because you are aware of areas in your life that are not pleasing to him. However, do you take full responsibility for what happened? Do you change in an attempt to be loved and accepted by your spouse?

16. Doubt – do you believe that you are capable of having your own opinion on matters? Do you feel as able to engage in rational thinking as your husband is? Can you think clearly about life decisions and what the Bible has to say about things.

17. Fear & worry – when you are anxious, what is it that you imagine might happen? What are you trying to prevent? How does this influence your day?

18. Guilt – when you feel guilty, what did you do that you believe is wrong?

19. Inhibition – in what way has your behavior around other people changed?

20. Anger – what goes on in your mind when you are angry? Who do you think about? What do you find unjust and wrong?

21. Shame – do you believe that there is something about you which means that others will not love or accept you? Why do you believe this is?

22. Changed mental state – in what ways has your ability to concentrate changed? What thoughts and memories are prominent in your thinking? Do you sense that your thinking has changed in a negative way? If so, in what sense?

23. Emotional, behavioral, and mental dependence – when you are thinking about your daily life, what goes on in your mind? Are you anticipating your husband's reaction? Are you second guessing him? What role does honoring the Lord play in what you think and do? What role does fear of your husband play in what you think and do? What role does love and acceptance play in what you think and do?

24. Depression and sorrow – when you experience sorrow, what is going on in your mind? What are you experiencing in your life that you wish was different? What has not turned out the way you thought things were supposed to? Which dreams that you held at the start have not happened?

3. God's Design for Marriage

ARLA'S DEEPEST DESIRE was to be a godly wife. To help her grow in her understanding of what the Bible teaches about who she is as a woman and how this is expressed in marriage, she asked an older lady in her church what the Bible teaches about the nature of women. The kind old lady took her to 1 Corinthians 11:7, explaining that her husband is the one made in the image of God, not her. Since she is her husband's glory, she is to follow and submit to him in all things, even if he expects her to sin, as he will be held accountable to God for both of them. Carla was confused by this teaching: Was it true that women are not made in the image of God? What about Genesis 1:26-28 where she read that both Adam and Eve are made in his image? Was she to go along with sin? What about Sapphira who died for telling the same lie as her husband? (Acts 5:1-11). Carla decided to explore further, asking other older men and women to explain what the Bible teaches on this topic.

Male and female in the image of God

Who are you? What does it mean to be human? What does it mean to be a woman? The first book of the

Bible, Genesis, explains these things to us. Let's look at Genesis 1.

Image of God in Genesis 1

In Genesis 1:26-28, we discover that in the beginning God deliberately chose to make human beings in his image. No other aspect of creation is described as being made in his image. Both the man and the woman were (and are) equal in this regard, and both are given the mandate by God to be fruitful, multiply, and rule over creation. The man and the woman are both equally blessed by God and have the same value and dignity.[10]

The Hebrew word for Adam is used to describe both Adam and Eve. And it describes the whole of humanity, not just the man or men.[11] We can see the equality of men and women as being made in the image of God again in Genesis 5:1-2; 9:6; and James 3:9.

We do not read in Genesis 1:26-28 what it *means* to be made in God's image, but we do read that they were both given dominion over the earth and commanded to be fruitful and multiply. This is the task they were both given to accomplish as creatures made in God's image – they are *not* a description of what it means to be made in that image. Practices in the Ancient Near East (ANE) can help us gain insight into a possible explanation of what this means. In the ANE, statues were constructed by kings as a representation of their power and reign in the far-off places of their realm. The statue represented the rule of the king in that entire area. An example of this is in Daniel 3:1 when King Nebuchadnezzar set up a statue of himself on the plain of Dura, in the province of Babylon. This statue represented his reign over Dura. Given this cultural practice at the time we can probably understand the meaning of the man and the woman being made in the image of God in Genesis 1 to include their role as joint representatives of God's rulership over his creation.[12]

Image of God in Genesis 2

In Genesis 2, we read about how both the man and the woman were specifically created. The creation of the woman is described in detail in Genesis 2:18-25. We discover that the woman was created from a rib of the man. Since Eve came from Adam's rib, she was his flesh and bones. She was created from the exact same substance as the man and was therefore just as fully human, just as fully created in the image of God as the man was.[13]

The woman was made to be the man's helper because it was not good for him to be alone (Genesis 2:18). When he saw the woman, he confirmed her similarity to him when he recognized that she is "bone of my bone and flesh of my flesh" (Genesis 2:23). The similarity is seen further because their relationship is described as 'one flesh' (Genesis 2:24). They were one flesh, of one nature, of the same kind. If she was less human than the man, bore less of God's image, or was made of a different substance than Adam, then they could not be described as 'one flesh'. This is how men and women today still bear the image of God.

The woman as Adam's helper

The woman was created to be a helper for the man (Genesis 2:18). The Hebrew word for "helper" means a help that is corresponding to the other, the man.[14] Elsewhere in the Old Testament, the same word is used in relation to the help that *God* gives to someone in need, or of the help that one nation could give to another in a time of need. The Lord is *your* helper! We can see this in Exodus 18:4; Deuteronomy 33:7, 26, 29; Psalm 20:2; 33:20; 70:5; 89:19; 115:9; 121:1; 124:8; 146:5; Isaiah 30:5; Ezekiel 12:14; Daniel 11:34, and Hosea 13:9.[15]

In the English language, the word "helper" can refer to a domestic servant or employee: someone inferior who serves someone who is his or her superior.[16] This is not the meaning of the Hebrew word. Since the word "helper" is a translation from a different language and culture, it is important that the English meaning of the word, in our time and culture, is not read back into the meaning of the biblical text. As we have read, God is called Israel's helper and nations helped other nations when it was necessary in their time of need. We can understand the term "helper" in the Bible to refer to a provider of strength that a person or a nation lacks in and of themselves.[17] In Genesis 2, the woman corresponds to the man and provides help that he lacks in and of himself. The word "helper" does not mean that the woman is less of a person than, or inferior to, the man.[18] Both the man and the woman are equally made in God's image.

The woman as the glory of the man

The difference between the man and the woman is addressed by Paul in 1 Corinthians 11:7. In this passage we read "For a man ought not to cover his head, since he is the image and glory of God, but woman is the glory of man." In this verse, Paul did not teach that the woman is made in the image of man, or that the woman is *not* made in the image of God.[19] In 1 Corinthians 11, Paul gives two reasons why the woman is the man's glory. The first reason is seen in verse 8. In this verse we read that it is because she *came from* the man. Paul is referring back to Genesis 2:22, where we read that God created the woman from the man.[20] The second reason is seen in verse 9. The woman is the man's glory because she was *created for* the man. We know from Genesis 2 that she was created for the man to be his helper. We looked at the correct meaning of this word already. According to 1 Corinthians 11:1-16, the woman being the glory of the man is seen in how she relates to him. A woman is to relate to her husband in a way that corresponds with the way that she was designed to, that is, by giving him honor.[21] The woman was made to honor God and to honor her husband.[22] In this passage the wives in the church in Corinth were taught to honor their husbands by covering their heads when they prayed or prophesied.

Polluted by sin

After sinning against God, Adam and Eve's relationship was polluted by sin. It is the same with all marriages since. We read about these consequences in Genesis 3:16: "Your desire shall be contrary to your husband, but he shall rule over you." But this verse must not be mistakenly taken as a command about how husbands and wives are supposed to relate to each other. It is describing the *consequences* of Adam and Eve's sin; it is not explaining how a husband and wife should behave. When teaching is given in the New Testament about marriage, Genesis 1 & 2 are often referred back to. These passages are Matthew 19:1-9; Ephesians 5:31; Mark 10:7-8; and 1 Corinthians 6:16.[23]

The Hebrew word translated in English as "desire" used of the wife in Genesis 3:16 occurs in two other places in the Old Testament: Genesis 4:7 and Song of Solomon 7:10. Song of Solomon 7:10 speaks of the man's *desire* for his lover. The difference between this passage and Genesis 3:16 is that the man's desire for his lover cannot be understood to be sinful.[24] In Genesis 4:7, like Genesis 3:16, both terms "desire" and "rule over" are used. In chapter 4, the words are used regarding sin's desire for Cain and the instruction that God gives him to rule over it. The woman's desire for her husband in Genesis 3:16 could therefore refer to a longing for relationship with him or to a desire to control him. The husband's rule over his wife is a consequence of his disobedience to God and involves him trying to dominate her.[25] The control and dominance spoken of in Genesis 3:16 are sinful distortions of how husbands and wives should relate to each other. Tyrannical abuse of position and turning responsibility into rights are a result of the fall.[26] These attitudes and behaviors should be repented of because they are sinful, even if normal in the culture we live in.

Christ the image of God

If we want to learn what it means to be God's image bearer, we can discover this by looking at Christ, the true image of God (2 Corinthians 4:4; Colossians 1:15; Hebrews 1:3; John 1:18; John 12:45; John 14:9). It is in Christ that we see a full reflection of God's character. Christ has renewed the image of God that was distorted by Adam (Colossians 3:9-11; 2 Corinthians 3:18; 1 Corinthians 15:49). This renewed image of God, when spoken of in the New Testament, is moral. Examples of some of the qualities involved in the renewed image of God include righteousness (Ephesians 4:24), purity (1 John 3:2, 3), love (1 John 3:10; 4:7), and forgiveness (Colossians 3:13).[27] The call to be renewed in the image of Christ is given to both men and women equally. It is a call to *all* believers.

Renewal in the image of God

The renewal of the image of God by the second Adam, Christ, was accomplished through his perfect obedience (Romans 5:12-21). He was obedient to the point of death on the cross, when he paid the penalty for Adam's sin. As a result, anyone who trusts Christ has died *with* him and therefore no longer has to answer for their sin. All believers are thus dead to the power of sin (Romans 6:6). It no longer has a hold over them. Having died to sin and been raised to life in Christ, the believer is to live for righteousness (Romans 6:12-14). This is true for all believers, male and female. Every believer approaches God through Christ alone and has access to God the Father through him alone. The Holy Spirit is given to all believers (Acts 2:17-18) and all receive spiritual gifts from him (1 Corinthians 12:7, 11; 1 Peter 4:10). All believers are made righteous, or justified, through Christ and are called sons of God (Galatians 3:26). The Greek term for 'sons' refers equally to men and women. Having been renewed in Christ, believers are called to become like him, who is the image of God (Colossians 1:15; 3:9-11; 2 Corinthians 3:18; 4:4). Every believer is called to be full of the Holy Spirit, to demonstrate the fruit of the Spirit (Ephesians 5:18; Galatians 5:22), to focus on the things above (Colossians 3:1-4), and to live according to the moral qualities of the new person in Christ that they now are (Colossians 3:12-17; Ephesians 4:17-32).

As a believer, you have access to God the Father through Christ, have the Holy Spirit indwelling you, have been given spiritual gifts, are called to become like Christ in your character, and are personally responsible for doing so. You have access to all the blessings in Christ (2 Peter 1:3, 4). This is your calling in life. Your husband should not prevent you from living for Christ, nor should you place pleasing him above this calling.

As your husband's helper, you are to help him become Christ-like. This includes speaking up and getting help regarding his sinful controlling behavior. By doing this, you are being obedient to the Lord and it is the most loving thing for him and your relationship. It is important that you do all that you can to prevent your husband treating you in an emotionally abusive way. "Christ…is the primary relationship in the life of a Christian, and no submission to any human being can be allowed to transgress that relationship. Thus, submission to another person should not require something that is incompatible with what Jesus requires."[28]

In marriage both the husband and the wife are to fulfil their responsibilities to each other. Husbands are to express their headship by loving their wives, and wives are to be submissive to their husbands (Colossians 3:18, 19; Ephesians 5:22-33). All other duties that are involved in the marital relationship are for the husband and wife equally. Paul does not teach husbands to rule their wives, rather they are to love them as Christ loved the church, and just as they love their own bodies.

If a husband uses his authority to make his wife do what he wants, he is using his power and authority sinfully.[29] It is opposed to Jesus' teaching to his disciples when he taught them to be servant-like rather than authoritarian and domineering (Matthew 20:25-28; Mark 10:42-45; Luke 22:25-26).

Submission

Meaning of the word

In the New Testament wives are instructed to submit to their husbands (Ephesians 5:22; Colossians 3:18-19; 1 Peter 3:1-7). The word translated as "submission" is the

Greek word *hupotassó* which means to be subject, to be subordinate.[30] The decision to submit is a voluntary act by the person themselves.[31] It is not something that can be forced on someone by the authority figure, someone to whom they have to be submissive.

The nature of submission

Ephesians 5:22 teaches that the wife is to submit to her husband as to the Lord. Similar teaching is found in Colossians 3:18. In Colossians, the wife's submission is to be as is fitting in the Lord. The motive for the wife's submission is obedience to the Lord.[32] Since the manner of submission is to be pleasing to Christ, submission should not be done for personal sinful reasons or due to sin on the part of the husband as neither of these correspond with what would be considered to be 'fitting in the Lord'.[33]

We read further in Ephesians 5:23-24 that since the husband is the head of the wife, she is to submit to him in everything, as the church submits to Christ. The term "in everything" expresses the comprehensiveness of the wife's submission. Her submission is to cover all areas of her life.[34] Paul is not teaching that the wife is to give into her husband's wishes about every single thing that he asks of her; for example, if he requires that she tell him every thought that she has throughout the day.

Peter instructs wives to be submissive to their husbands, even if the husband is not obedient to the Word (1 Peter 3:1-6). By doing so, her behavior is a witness to him.[35] In the culture at the time when

Peter wrote his letter, women were expected to follow the religion of their fathers, or after marriage, of their husbands. The fact that a Christian wife was not following the religion of her husband would be seen as rebellion against her husband's authority by the society around her.[36] This shows that a wife is to follow the Lord above other people around her, and that she is to do this while leading a holy life. By being submissive to her husband in her day-to-day life, she shows appropriate respect to her non-believing husband.[37] Even though following a different religion than her husband would be seen as disrespectful, her behavior toward him should demonstrate that she does give him appropriate respect.

Wrong ideas regarding submission

Since submission is a voluntary subjection to an authority above a person, it does not mean that you are not to think critically, i.e. evaluate how you live your life.[38] You are responsible before the Lord for your mind. As your husband's helper, it is necessary that you think biblically as you will be able to help him in a way that is honoring to the Lord.

Your submission to your husband should not be absolute, nor should you submit to sin.[39] It also does not mean that you are to subject your whole self to your husband, that you allow "slavery or tyrannical authority," or that you allow the breaking of your will.[40] Neither should submission be used as the basis on which the rest of your behavior is based.[41] Your first calling is to glorify the Lord in your thinking and behavior. From that calling flows submission to your husband. It does not mean that you are first submissive to your husband and then operate out of that. Examples of people who refused to submit to the sinful instructions of those in authority over them are the Hebrew midwives (Exodus 1:17); Esther regarding Xerxes (Esther 4:16); Shadrach, Meshach, and Abednego (Daniel 3:13-18); Daniel (Daniel 6:10-14); the apostles (Acts 4:18-20; 5:27-29); and Moses' parents (Hebrews 11:23). Sapphira was submissive to her husband by telling the same lie that he told to the other believers (Acts 5:1-11). Even though she was following a person in authority above her, she was held personally accountable for telling a lie and was punished by death in the same way as her husband was. Both Ananias and Sapphira were held individually responsible for their own behavior and received the same judgment and punishment for lying to the Holy Spirit.

When Peter uses Sarah's submission as an example for Christian wives to follow, he cannot be referring to the times when she lied as instructed by her husband (Genesis 12:10-20; 20:1-7). This is because Peter instructs wives to do good. Submitting to sin would mean that the wife was being complicit in doing evil, as in the case of Sapphira, rather than doing good.

Christ the ultimate authority

Since your submission to your husband is to be as is fitting in the Lord (Colossians 3:18), this assumes that you are already submitted to Christ. Christ is to be the ultimate authority in your life, not your husband. As we've seen, Sapphira was held personally accountable for her words before the Lord (Acts 5:1-11). Her husband's authority did not replace her own individual responsibility to obey God.

Headship

Meaning of the word

Paul teaches in Ephesians 5:23 that a husband is the head of his wife. The Greek word translated as head is *kephalē*. It is assumed in this book that the husband being the head of his wife means that he has a position of authority over her.

The responsibility to love

There are three passages in the New Testament which speak about how a husband should treat his wife. These passages are 1 Peter 3:7, Ephesians 5:25-33, and Colossians 3:19. All three teach the importance of the loving care that the husband is to provide for his wife.

In 1 Peter 3:7, Peter instructs husbands to live with their wives in an understanding way, which involves showing honor to her as the weaker partner. Both Ephesians 5:25-33 and Colossians 3:19 instruct husbands to love their wives. Colossians adds that husbands are not to be harsh with them.

Paul elaborates on the kind of love the husband is to give his wife in Ephesians 5:25-33. He is to sacrificially give of himself to her, nourishing and cherishing her, for her good. His love should be like the love that Christ has for the church.

In Ephesians, Paul commands husbands to love their wives as their own bodies. The wife is said to be part of his body as the church is the body of Christ. When the husband loves his wife, he is also loving himself. This connection between a husband and a wife is formed because they are no longer two, but one flesh (5:31). Since the husband is one flesh with his wife, it is in his own best interest to care for her.

The responsibility to imitate Christ

Paul teaches in Ephesians 5:25 that husbands are to imitate Christ in how they love their wives. Christ loved others by serving and dying for them (John 13:1-17; 1 John 3:16). If the husband has Christ-like love for his wife, he will have the good of his wife as his objective. The assertive and crushing behavior involved in emotional abuse has no place in how a Christian husband should relate to his wife.

Headship does not mean ruling forcefully

Husbands are *not* taught to have authority over their wives, nor to *ensure* that their wives submit to them. The authority that husbands have is derived from God and should therefore be practiced in a way that is subject to Scripture and honors God. Jesus taught his disciples that the use of authority that honors him is that of being a servant. He forbade his disciples from ruling over others (Mark 10:42-45).

Therefore, it is sinful for a husband to relate to his wife in order to have power over her. It is sinful to forbid things that the Bible commands, as this goes against the teaching of Scripture. It is also sinful if he forbids her from reading her Bible, having fellowship with others, attending church, or thinking in a biblical way.[42] Supervising the details of her life is not headship as the Lord intends, nor is self-centeredness or self-assertion.[43]

Debbie's story

Debbie came to understand that men and women were made deliberately by God to reflect himself and his rulership over creation. The woman was created from the man to be his helper and glory. Being made from the man means that the woman is of the same substance as him. As Pete's helper, she began to appreciate that she can provide strength that he lacks in himself and is to help him reflect the image of God. She also understood that their relationship dynamics had been marred by the fall into sin, and that there was now a power struggle in relationships. Debbie was thrilled to read that Christ's death and resurrection have renewed the image of God in men and women that was marred by sin. Being dead to sin and alive to righteousness, both Pete and Debbie are called to reflect Christ. They are each responsible for their own individual obedience to him, with Christ the ultimate authority over both of them.

Debbie began to realize that she is to submit to her husband out of love and obedience to Christ, which is a voluntary choice on her part. While having an attitude of submission and respect toward Pete in all areas of her life, she did not need to submit to sin, be complicit in it, tolerate her husband treating her in a sinful way, or allow him to control her thinking or behavior. She also better understood that Pete is called to love her as Christ loved the church, seeing her as his own body and respecting her as the weaker vessel. He is not to exercise dominion over her but to serve and love her as Christ does the church.

Questions for Reflection

1. As you think about who you are as a person, what do you believe to be your identity? How do you see yourself?

2. Read Genesis 1:26-28. Who does God say that you are? Is there any difference in value or dignity between you and your husband?

3. According to this chapter, what does being made in God's image involve?

4. What are the implications of the woman coming from the man's rib?

5. Is what way is the woman similar to the man in Genesis 2?

6. What does the term "helper" mean according to the Bible? How does this compare to how you under-stand your role toward your husband?

7. What are the reasons given in 1 Corinthians 11:7 for why a wife is her husband's glory? What does Paul *not* teach about the nature of the wife? Is the wife in any sense inferior to her husband?

8. Read Genesis 3:16. This passage describes the consequences of the fall into sin. It is not a command about how to behave. As you honestly reflect on your relationship with your husband, in what way do you let a desire for relationship or for control over him influence you? In what ways does he rule over you?

9. Read Colossians 3:9-11, 2 Corinthians 3:18, and 1 Corinthians 15:49. What does the Lord call you to do?

10. Read Romans 6:1-14. List what Christ has done. List what this means for you. How does the Lord call you to live? Having read these verses, what is your first calling in life?

11. What does it mean for you to help your husband to become Christ-like? As you honestly reflect on your life, in what ways do you relate to him that are not helping him to become more like Christ? What does this mean when he behaves sinfully toward you?

12. Read Ephesians 5:22, Colossians 3:18-19, and 1 Peter 3:1-7 (as well as the surrounding passages to understand the context). Who makes the choice to be submissive? What is the motive for that submission? Since submission comes from obedience to the Lord, what motives for submission does this *exclude*? What does this mean for your ability to think critically? Who is the ultimate

authority for your life, to whom are you responsible for all your thoughts, motives, and behavior?

13. Read 1 Peter 3:7, Ephesians 5:25-33, and Colossians 3:19 (as well as the surrounding passages to understand the context). What do these passages teach that headship involves? How is a husband to treat his wife? Whose headship are husbands to imitate as they relate to their wives? What kind of behavior does this exclude?

4. Living for Christ

LINDA HAD ALWAYS been told that for her husband Bill to change, she was to pray for him, submit to him, and not complain. By submitting and praying, he would change. After 30 years of marriage, she knew there must be more to being a Christian woman in her situation. She wanted to know how to live in a way that would glorify God. While wanting to be obedient to the Lord, and submissive to Bill, she noticed that when she submitted to him in absolutely everything that he asked his treatment of her got worse, as did his control over her life. She wondered if she was understanding submission properly. She also wondered how to be wise about the role of the church and other believers in her life. Linda struggled regularly with anger, worry, and loneliness. She wanted to know how she could experience change in these areas.

Our purpose in life is to glorify christ

Paul goes to great lengths to teach us in Romans that all believers are called to live for righteousness (Romans 6:12-14). Regardless of a believer's circumstances, their purpose in life is to live for the glory of God. That is our calling and purpose. We have been saved from alienation and hostility in our minds in order to be holy and blameless before God (Colossians 1:21, 22), we are chosen to be holy and blameless before him (Ephesians 1:4), we are to be conformed to the image of God's Son (Romans 8:29), and we are called to obey the Lord (1 Peter 1:2).

Our identity is in Christ

We are renewed in Jesus and called to live for his glory. Our identity is in him, which includes being:

- Blessed in Christ with every spiritual blessing in the heavenly places (Ephesians 1:3)
- Chosen before the foundation of the world to be holy and blameless (Ephesians 1:4)
- Predestined for adoption (Ephesians 1:5)
- Redeemed through his blood and forgiven of sin (Ephesians 1:7)
- The recipient of an inheritance (Ephesians 1:11)
- Predestined to be to the praise of his glory (Ephesians 1:11)
- Sealed with the Holy Spirit as a guarantee of the inheritance (Ephesians 1:13, 14)
- Complete in Christ (Colossians 2:10)

Wise submission

Wives are instructed in Scripture to be submissive to their husbands in a way that is fitting in the Lord (Ephesians 5:22; Colossians 3:18-19; 1 Peter 3:1-7). As we have seen, the word translated as "submission" is the Greek word *hupotassō,* which means to be subject, to be subordinate.[44] Submission is a voluntary act by the person themselves and should not be forced upon someone.[45] Since Scripture never contradicts Scripture, i.e. God's Word is consistent throughout,[46] submission to your husband cannot involve submission to sin nor to you being prevented from living according to your purpose of glorifying Christ.[47]

As we have seen, you are responsible and accountable to God for your thoughts and behavior. You should never give this responsibility to another person by allowing them to control you or your thinking. In an emotionally abusive relationship the husband uses things such as fear, guilt, shame, insinuations, and accusations in order to control his wife. If you go along with this, it will result in your living in fear, guilt, shame, and believing falsehoods about yourself. These heart issues belong to the old nature, Christ has redeemed you to live as the new person you are in him. It is contrary to your calling to accept emotionally abusive behavior.

What will probably be surprising to you is that if you accept abusive behaviors such as anger, (veiled) threats, jealousy, and punishments, you are inadvertently enabling your husband to live according to his old nature. As his God-given helper called to help him reflect

Jesus, you are actually obeying the Lord if you seek godly help from others. It is important that you know that you are *not responsible* for ensuring that he is happy and not angry or jealous. He is responsible before God, and will have to give an account to Him for his own thoughts, emotions, and behavior.

> **It is contrary to your calling to accept emotionally abusive behavior.**

If you are experiencing emotional abuse, your husband is probably trying to control you in areas that are not explicitly taught about in Scripture. For example, he may demand that you answer an email within five minutes after he has sent it, immediately answer a text or other message on social media, or scrutinize how you use the minutes of your day. Wisdom is needed to know how to respond in such situations. You could ask "If I do this, where will it lead to, what will it result in?" For example, if it leads to him controlling you by not allowing you to go out of the house, it is probably wise that you do not go along with his demand because you will not be fulfilling your responsibilities to others to be a blessing to them. You will also not be able to be the person you should be toward the rest of the family.

Heart issues

What the heart is

The Bible uses different Greek words inter-changeably to describe the inner person.[48] These can be translated as heart, mind, soul, conscience, inner self, and inner man.[49] We will summarize these references for the inner person by using the word "heart." The word "heart" refers to the core of a person, that is, to his or her character. It is the non-physical part of what it means to be human.[50] The heart of a person is where his or her thoughts, will, speech, and attitudes originate.[51] It is our moral center and where we decide whether we will live for God, who we will worship, and who we will love.[52]

What heart change is

Whatever is going on in your heart will determine how you function. Jesus teaches in Mark 7:21-23 that whatever comes out of your heart defiles you. It is what you are thinking in your heart that determines your response to the abuse.

Are you like a lot of women in emotionally abusive marriages, for who peace in the home is one of the most important priorities in their lives, even if this means tolerating evil on the part of their husbands? You may crave to be loved so much that you will endure your husband's abusive behavior, hoping that by doing so you will win his love, or you might believe that you can no longer handle your situation and give up. You will have built patterns of thinking and behavior based on what you have thought in your heart when your husband treated you in an abusive way.

Living according to your purpose involves having the mind of Christ. Up until now, you might have accepted what your husband told you. To think in ways that honor the Lord will involve testing any accusations, insinuations, exaggerations, twisting of facts, and/or use of guilt by what the Bible teaches about who Jesus is, what he says about you, and what he says about how you should live. After testing these things, it is very important that you believe and apply biblical teaching on these matters in your life.

There are a number of heart issues that you might struggle with. Jesus has answers for each of these issues in Scripture!

Confusion and doubt

Understanding that you are to have the mind of Christ will help you come out of the state of confusion and doubt that you have been in. Instead of blindly believing whatever accusations your husband makes about how bad you are, you can live in and through Jesus. This will help you better discern when he tries to shift blame onto you. If he denies having done or said something which he *did* say or do, it will help you not to accept his denial as being the truth.

A husband who switches from being loving and charming to being angry and cruel can come to lose his hold over you. Your motive will no longer be to try to ensure that he starts treating you kindly or try to stop his cruel behavior, because your motive is to live and relate to him in a way that honors Jesus. In time it is possible that you will no longer be susceptible to his mind-games, will stop second-guessing how he will respond to you, will no longer doubt your own ability to perceive reality as a human being, and will no longer continue to blame yourself for everything. This will lead to your husband no longer being able to control your thinking.

Worry

Worry involves being preoccupied with or "overly concerned" about something.[53] The main New Testament passages that address the issue of worry are Matthew 6:19-36 and Philippians 4:4-9.

Biblical instruction for dealing with worry

Matthew 6:19-36 instructs us not lay up treasure on earth. We are to lay up treasure in heaven where it cannot be destroyed. You and I can discover what our treasure is by finding out what it is that we worry about. You might be tempted to worry about how to ensure that your husband is not angry with you, other people, or things in life that do not work out as he desires. You might worry about how to gain his love and acceptance, how you could survive (both mentally and financially) if he left you, and about your children suffering if he chose to punish them because he's angry with you (or them) for some reason.

This passage teaches that you are not to worry because God cares for his creation. Since you are much more valuable than the birds and flowers of creation that God cares for, you can be certain that he will take care of you. Thankfully, he also shows you what to focus on instead of worrying. You are called to seek God's kingdom first. This means putting God's reign, his rule first in our lives, praying for his kingdom to come, his reign to impact those we come into contact with or who God has laid on our hearts to pray for.

Philippians 4:4-9 instructs believers to rejoice in the Lord, not to be anxious but to be prayerful, and to think of ways that honor God. To help you rejoice in the Lord you could make a list of God's attributes and think about how a particular aspect of who God is relates to whatever you are worrying about. You could also write down what God has done in your life up until the present day. Seeing the way in which he has cared for you and worked in your life in the past will help reassure you that the Lord will keep his promises in relation to your concerns about the present and the future.

It is possible to learn to pray about these issues in a thankful way. Your thankfulness is toward the Lord because you know that he will care for you. When you do this, God promises that his peace will guard your mind and heart. Peter gives similar teaching. He instructs believers to "humble yourselves, therefore, under the mighty hand of God so that at the proper time he may exalt you, casting all your anxieties on him, because he cares for you" (1 Peter 5:6, 7).

To help think about what is true, honorable, just, pure, lovely, commendable, excellent, and praiseworthy (Philippians 4:8), you could make a list of the thoughts that you have when you worry and ask yourself if these thoughts correspond with the kind of thoughts described in this verse. It is helpful to then think about how God's attributes and promises are true regarding those specific issues that you are worrying about.

Here are some of God's attributes. He is:

- Omnipresent – he is everywhere (Jeremiah 23:23-24; Psalm 139:7-10)
- Omniscient – he knows everything (1 John 3:20; Psalm 139:1-2, 4, 16)
- Wise (Romans 16:27; 1 Corinthians 1:24, 30; Ephesians 3:10)
- Faithful (Deuteronomy 32:4)
- Good (Luke 18:19; Psalm 100:5; Psalm 106:1; Psalm 107:1; Psalm 34:8)
- Loving (1 John 4:8; John 3:16; Galatians 2:20)
- Merciful (2 Corinthians 1:3)
- Gracious (Romans 3:24; 2 Corinthians 8:9; Ephesians 2:8)
- Holy (Psalm 71:22; 78:41; 89:18; Isaiah 1:4; 5:19, 24; 6:3; 1 Peter 1:16)
- Righteous (Deuteronomy 32:4),
- Jealous (Exodus 34:14; Deuteronomy 4:24; 5:9)
- Full of wrath (Exodus 32:9-10;

Deuteronomy 9:7-8; 29:23; 2 Kings 22:13; Romans 1:18)
- Omnipotent – he is all powerful (Psalm 24:8; Genesis 18:14; Jeremiah 32:27; Revelation 1:8)
- Longsuffering/patient (Exodus 34:6; Psalm 86:15; Romans 2:4; 9:22; 1 Peter 3:20; 2 Peter 3:15)[54]

Fear

You might be fearful of what your husband might do to you and be afraid of speaking about him in a negative way to others. You could be afraid of speaking to your church leaders about the way he is treating you. Many women believe that they would be disloyal to their husbands if they were to tell others.

The fear that you experience may be the result of direct or veiled threats that he has made toward you, or what you imagine might happen to you if you were to upset him too much. Anyone who lives in fear becomes paralyzed from taking action. If you are dependent on him both mentally and financially, you could fear being rejected or abandoned by him because you think you would not be able to survive without him.

Fear of man

The fear of man is "any anxiety that is caused by real or imagined discomfort, rejection, or danger being imposed on another human being."[55] It involves trying to ensure that we do not upset people more than being concerned about honoring God. It is an "inordinate desire for people's approval" or an "inordinate fear of their rejection."[56] People who fear others will study their body language, likes and dislikes. They are unlikely to question the views of others and will react to conflict by giving in, withdrawing, or steering the conversation onto another topic.

Fear of God

If you fear man, you will probably struggle to fear God. Knowing who God is conquers the fear of man. Understanding his providence over believers is important. God's providence is as follows:

"God is continually involved with all created things in such a way that he (1) keeps them existing and maintaining the properties with which he created them; (2) cooperates with created things in every action, directing their distinctive properties to cause them to act as they do; and (3) directs them to fulfil his purposes."[57]

God is directing all things to fulfil his purposes. He is in control and working according to his plan in your life. Ultimately, your husband is not in control.

Fearing God includes the knowledge that you are by nature unclean and deserve to be punished by a holy God. It also includes the knowledge that because you have trusted Jesus you have been made righteous by him. Understanding the work of Jesus on the cross will lead you to worship and trust him.[58]

Trusting the God of Scripture

In the Bible we discover that fear originated in Genesis 3:7-8 when Adam and Eve hid from each other and from God after they had disobeyed his command not to eat from the tree of the knowledge of good and evil. Later the people of Israel gave in to fear when they saw the giants of the land; they did not trust that God could lead them into the Promised Land (Numbers 13). In Deuteronomy, God tells Moses not to be afraid of Og King of Bashan, because God had already given him into Moses' hand (Deuteronomy 3:2). Moses instructed Joshua not to fear the other nations because the Lord would fight for him, and told the people of Israel not to be afraid of the nations (Deuteronomy 3:22). Instead of being fearful, they were to remember what the Lord did to Pharaoh (Deuteronomy 7:17-18). Joshua was commanded not to be afraid of the nations because the Lord was with him (Joshua 1:9). He then instructed the chiefs of the men of war not to be afraid but to be courageous, because the Lord would help them against their enemies (Joshua 10:25).

David wrote about fear in many of his Psalms. For example in Psalm 23:4 he wrote that he feared no evil because the Lord was with him: God's rod and staff brought David comfort. In Psalm 27:1-2 we read that David refused to be afraid of his enemies because the Lord was his light, salvation, and stronghold. In Psalm 3, although David knew that his enemies surrounded him, he trusted the Lord as his protector.

In Jeremiah 17:5-8, the person who trusts in other

people is described as someone who will suffer and not prosper. In contrast, the person who trusts the Lord will be blessed and lead a fruitful life.

You can trust the God who is with you, cares for you, protects you, and is providentially bringing about his plan for your life. This will help you when you are tempted to fill your mind with fearful thoughts of what your husband might do, or what might or might not happen if you were to behave in some way that would upset him too much.

Guilt

Does your husband blame you for his own sin, failures and guilt, not just yours? If you accept the blame for these areas in *his* life, you will come to believe, as he already does, that if you had not said or done certain things, he would not have treated you in the way that he did. Since you are not the cause of his behavior, you are also not the solution for bringing about change in his thoughts, emotions, or behavior.

The Importance of justification

It is really important that you understand the work of Jesus on the cross. The Bible teaches that you are by nature a sinner who deserves to be punished (Romans 3:10, 23) but through Jesus' death on the cross you have been made righteous before God (2 Corinthians 5:21; Romans 3:24; 8:30). You are called to live on the basis of this righteous standing before God. Since you are in

Christ, there is now no condemnation for you (Romans 8:1). You can reject this kind of condemning speech from your husband because God has justified you, and Christ is seated at the right hand of God and is interceding for you (Romans 8:33, 34).

> *Since you are not the cause of his behavior, you are also not the solution for bringing about change in his thoughts, emotions, or behavior.*

The role of sanctification

Being justified in Christ, you are to become like him in your character. This involves putting off the old self, renewing your thinking, and putting on the new self, created after the righteousness of God (Ephesians 4:22-24). If you are harboring, for example, anger, malice, strife, or jealousy in your heart (Colossians 3:8; Galatians 5:20; 1 Peter 2:1), it is important to understand that these belong to the old nature, and that you can repent of these heart attitudes.

Experiencing guilt for these things is the way that the Lord uses to bring about change in our lives. Since God is *for* you in Christ, if you confess these sinful heart attitudes, you will be forgiven by him. He is your Advocate with the Father who is faithful and just (1 John 1:9-2:3).

At the same time, you should not accept

condemnation from your husband since Jesus died to take away your condemnation and is for you. By repenting of your personal sin, guilt is removed from your life. If you accept his accusations or insinuations as being true, or take the blame for his mistreatment of you, you will live in guilt. The reason for this is because you are not the cause of his behavior. Since you are not the cause of his behavior, you are also not the solution for bringing about change in his thoughts, emotions, or behavior.

Anger

Women in emotionally abusive relationships often struggle with anger. Anger is "a response by the whole person of negative moral judgment against perceived evil."[59] Although the temptation to anger is a reaction to the way that your husband treats you, any sinful anger on your part comes from out of your own heart. It involves both mental judgment of perceived evil and an emotional response to that evil.

The anger of God

Not all anger is sinful. We read in the Bible that God can be angry and exercise judgment. For example he was angry with Moses when he asked that someone else lead Israel out of Egypt (Exodus 4:14). The psalmist warns against making the Son angry (Psalm 2:12). Jesus was angry when he saw people making a profit at the temple instead of it being a place of worship (John 2:13-17). His anger was due to the sin of the people.

Human righteous anger

People can also experience righteous anger. This is due to a sense of justice that people have because they are made in the image of a just God. When we see injustice, we want to see justice happen. However, in order for anger to be righteous, it must involve the following: (1) a sin that has occurred; (2) a concern for the glory of God, not one's own glory; and (3) a righteous expression of that anger. For example, talking to the person who provoked you to anger about what happened in a way that addresses the issues involved, seeks mutual understanding, and does not attack the other person.[60]

Human sinful anger

Human anger is usually sinful, and flows out of our heart, which is naturally corrupt. James 4:1-3 teaches that anger comes from thwarted desires: you cannot get what you want. The underlying attitude of the angry person is that they want something, need something, or are convinced that they deserve something. The angry person wants something so much that they are willing to sin in order to get it, and to sin because they do not have it. Anger is usually a sinful response to not getting what one desires or longs for (James 1:13-15).

Dealing with your angry heart

Any anger you experience comes from your own heart. Understanding this and working on what is going on in your heart will mean that you can live differently in your situation. We are called to conquer our anger (Proverbs 16:32; 25:28; James 1:19; Proverbs 22:24-25; Ephesians 4:31-32). Gaining insight into exactly what it is that you desire so much will help you deal with your anger.

- You can discover this by asking a few questions:
- What circumstances led to my becoming angry?
- What did I say and do when I became angry?
- What did I say to myself when I became angry?
- What do I want from other people?

You may desire to be respected, for your husband not to order you around, to show you love, be less angry at you, control his speech, acknowledge wrongdoing in his past, or to have fewer mood swings.

Change comes as you admit that these desires, which are good in themselves, have been controlling you. This is extremely difficult to do, although possible with the Lord's enabling. After answering the questions above, you will probably see patterns when you become angry. For example, you might become angry when you see your husband speaking to other people in a respectful way. You will also see that your thoughts go beyond the incident itself to thinking angrily about your husband and maybe the others involved. The answers will show you how you typically express your anger in what you say and do. From here you can plan ahead about what to think when you are in similar situations in the future. It is very helpful to think about truths in Scripture. 1 Peter is full of truths for people who are suffering at the hands of others. While filling your mind with truths, you could find ways of regaining self-control so that you are not expressing your anger in wrong or sinful ways. An example is exercising, such as going for a walk or using an indoor bike.

Shame

A person experiences shame as a result of thinking that he or she is a failure. If you are experiencing shame, it could be because you believe that you are unable to live up to your husband's standards: you believe there is something wrong with you.

Since the shame is due to some kind of perceived failure on your part, you will never be able to achieve the desired standards he has for you – you believe that by nature you are inadequate. Your shame can also be because of your own behavior, something that was done to you by other people, or something about you which your husband believes makes you inferior to him; for example he might believe that you are inferior simply because you are a woman.

Shame in the Bible

We first see shame in the Bible in Genesis 3:7 when Adam and Eve covered themselves because they were naked. This is in contrast to Genesis 2:25 when Adam and Eve experienced no shame about being naked during the period of innocence before the fall in Genesis 3. The human experience of shame is a result of the guilt of sinning against God. The shame of nakedness is seen again in 2 Samuel 10:4, when Hanun shamed David's men by stripping them of their clothes and shaving off their beards. In this case, the shame experienced was a result of a deliberate attempt by Hanun's men to humiliate David's men.

Christ removes shame

Christ is the answer for the shamed person. In the gospels we see that Jesus associated with those who were shamed by others because they were seen to be inferior. Examples are the woman at the well (John 4:1-45) and the tax collectors and sinners (Matthew 9:9-13). By dying on the cross Jesus died in a shameful way, being naked and exposed to everybody who was looking at him. He fulfilled Isaiah 53:3-5, knowing the shame of being "as one from whom men hide their faces, he was despised, and we esteemed him not." Even though he was innocent, he suffered shame so that others would be made righteous. Through his death and resurrection on the cross, Jesus canceled the debt that is against you and me (Colossians 2:14). As a result of Jesus' death on the cross when he became sin, you and I have become the righteousness of God (2 Corinthians 5:21). We have been justified by faith through Christ (Romans 5:1). There is now no condemnation for anyone in Christ

Jesus, we are to live according to God's plan for our lives, being holy and blameless before Him (Romans 8:1; Ephesians 1:4).

(Un)Ashamed

You are righteous in Christ because of his work on the cross. Your shame has been borne by him so that you can live a godly life. Your alienation from God has been removed by Jesus so that you may be holy and blameless before him (Colossians 1:21, 22).

Instead of accepting your husband's judgment of you, look to how Jesus sees you. By nature, you are a sinner who does not match God's perfect standard and are cut off from him. But as a believer, you have been clothed with the righteousness of Christ because of his work on the cross. You belong to Christ, even if your husband rejects and excludes you! Jesus has removed your shame in a personal, intimate way. In Isaiah 54:4-6 the Lord comforts Israel by saying that she is to forget her shame as he, her Maker, is her husband. This is true of the church, the bride of Christ (Revelation 21:1-4). And you are part of the bride of Christ, in him you are holy and without blemish (Ephesians 5:27).

Jesus is the answer for the shamed person.

Loneliness

Loneliness is an emotionally painful sense of not being connected to others. If you are feeling lonely, it may involve feelings of being unwanted, isolated, and left out. Your loneliness may be the result of living in fear, being isolated from others, a lack of intimacy with God, a lack of emotional connection with others, and a sense of being rejected by your husband.

Examples of loneliness in the Bible

There are many examples of lonely people in the Bible. In 1 Kings 19:10 Elijah was in a state of great distress. He believed that he was left alone to serve the Lord. We also see in Scripture where David's soul waited in silence for God alone. He knew that his hope was only in him (Psalm 62:5). There was no other person who took notice of him or took care of his soul (Psalm 142:4). Asaph had no one on earth or heaven besides God (Psalm 73:25, 26). Demas, Crescens, and Titus left Paul, it was only the Lord who stood by him during his first trial (2 Timothy 4:10, 16, 17). Those closest to Jesus deserted him (Mark 14:50), Peter denied him (John 18:15-18; 25-27), and Judas betrayed him (Matthew 26:47-50). He was alone during his suffering in the Garden of Gethsemane (Matthew 26:36-46) and was forsaken by the Father when he hung on the cross (Matthew 27:46).[61]

Dealing with loneliness

It is important to be connected to others. God has promised believers throughout the ages that he will neither leave them nor forsake them, he will always be with them (Psalm 139:7-12; Isaiah 41:10; Matthew

28:20; Hebrews 13:5). You can experience intimacy with God by living and trusting that *he* is your husband. He compared his people in the Old Testament to a young wife who is deserted and grieved in spirit, a young woman rejected by her husband (Isaiah 54:5, 6). We read in Hosea that despite this, God betrothed his people to him in righteousness, justice, steadfast love, mercy, and faithfulness (Hosea 2:19, 20). Believers continue to be described as the bride of Christ in the New Testament (Ephesians 5:31, 32; Revelation 21:2).

To overcome loneliness, it will also be important to establish relationships with other people. This will probably displease your husband as coming out of your isolation will result in him having less control over you. This calls for wisdom about who you spend time with, and when.

Depression

If you are experiencing depression, you will probably believe that nothing in life has any sense or purpose. You may start to think doing anything is pointless. You may find getting out of bed in the morning difficult. You may lack hope, think negatively, and see the worst in situations and people.

Dealing with the your heart of depression

Perhaps your loss of hope is linked to your husband not giving the love, respect, acceptance, and kindness that you long for and expected in marriage. And this may be despite years of adapting and living according to his standards, views, and desires. It could be that these desires and your attempts to win the love of your husband and his trust has superseded the place of the Lord in your life.

Knowing Jesus as the purpose in life

You have life-giving hope because, in Christ, you have received everything that you need to live in a godly way (2 Peter 1:3, 4). You now know the Father of all compassion and the God of all comfort (2 Corinthians 1:3, 4). It is possible to regain hope in life because you know that the God of hope desires that you live in hope and that he can use your suffering for good (Romans 15:4; 5:1-5).

> *You belong to Jesus, even if your husband rejects and excludes you.*

It is important to think about what is true and to focus on the Lord. It is helpful to write down things that you can think about when you are tempted to think sad thoughts. You can ask your Christian friends to help you think according to who God is, what he has done for you, and what he has promised. As you work on these things, begin working on your use of time, starting with doing *one* responsible thing every day, you can then move on later to being able to follow a schedule for the whole week. This scheduling should include set times for getting up in the morning and going to bed at night, eating healthily, and exercising.

You belong to Jesus, even if your husband rejects and excludes you.

Honoring Christ in the home

Speech

In Genesis 1, we read that God spoke creation into being (Genesis 1:3, 6, 9, 11, 14, 20, 24, 26). He gave human beings the ability to speak which Adam used when he named the animals in Genesis 2 and exclaimed "bone of my bones and flesh of my flesh" when he was introduced to Eve.

Satan manipulated words, in this case God's, when he spoke to Eve and questioned if God really did say that she should not eat of any tree in the garden. He then went on to claim that Adam and Eve would be like God, knowing good and evil if they ate from the tree of the knowledge of good and evil. As a result of Adam and Eve's decision to listen to Satan and disobey God and eat from the tree, human speech is affected by sin. We immediately see this when Adam and Eve then blamed each other and God for their own behavior (Genesis 3: 12, 13).

Our speech should be for the glory of Christ and the good of the other person (Colossians 4:6; Ephesians 4:29). The language that we speak comes out of our hearts (Mark 7:20-23; Matthew 12:34). By letting the Lord work on your heart, you will be enabled to speak in an appropriate way to your husband, which humanly speaking seems like an impossible thing to do.

If he verbally attacks you, you could say to him that you want to communicate with him in a calm and productive way, not in an aggressive manner. You could ask him to stop speaking to you in an attacking way. If he continues to do so, you could repeat what you have just said and add that you will leave the room if he does not stop. If he refuses to stop verbally attacking you, you should leave the room. If he continues attacking you, you could even leave the house. It is important that you create physical distance. If you are discussing an issue with your husband and starts to verbally attack, accuse, blame, or divert the conversation onto something else, instead of being diverted, becoming defensive, or retaliating, it is important to stick to the issue being discussed by repeating what you were talking about in a polite and calm way.

All believers are called to care for one another and to confront fellow believers who are sinning (Galatians 6:1; Matthew 18:15), so it is right for you to confront your husband when he is sinning against you as he claims that he is a believer. Being passive and not confronting sin will make it easier for him to continue to mistreat you. By confronting him about his sin, you are truly helping him because you are addressing issues in his life that do not correspond to the character of Jesus.

Boundaries

Preventing your husband from speaking to you in a harsh, angry, accusatory, or attacking manner (or from behaving in a way that punishes, harms, or attempts to intimidate you) is a way of setting boundaries around how you allow him to treat you. This is not selfish self-protection because you are setting limits to ensure he is less able to treat you in a way that is according to the old nature (Colossians 3:5-12; Galatians 5:19-21). You are helping your husband by seeking to prevent him from engaging in ungodly behavior. At the same time, you are seeking to think and behave in ways that honor the Lord.

If he counters your ideas or feelings, it is important not to try to explain or attempt to get him to understand. In my long experience in counseling women in these sorts of situations, what will likely happen is that he will just counter your explanation and argue back at you. You should simply repeat what you said. If he discounts what you say, you can say that you want your communication to honor the Lord.

Emotional abusers often make comments by joking. If he speaks in this way, you should *not* explain why you don't think his joke was funny, because he will probably argue with you about your reasons, say that those reasons are foolish, and claim that you need to loosen up or that there is something wrong with you. When he denies that he has said certain things or treated you in a certain way, try not try to explain to him what happened in an attempt to make him remember or understand. Why? He probably does understand and knows what happened.

> *Emotional abusers often make comments by joking.*

Also, if you believe him when he denies things or counters you, you will probably begin to question your ability to perceive events and circumstances.[62] In other words, don't get into an argument or long discussion as it will not help you, or him.

Doing good

Another way of honoring the Lord is in how you respond to your husband. An important motivating desire is to avoid being overcome by evil, but to overcome evil with good (Romans 12:21). If you deal with the issues of your own heart, it will help ensure that you are not overcome by evil. By doing good toward your husband, you are overcoming his evil with good.

Peter teaches this in 1 Peter 3:8-17. Instead of responding to evil with evil and put downs and insults with put downs and insults, you should seek to bless him. This is only possible by the grace of God and the power of the Holy Spirit. In this way you will experience the Lord's blessing in your life. Good deeds include doing your daily tasks and seeking to be a blessing to others. Other people include your husband, your children, and people outside the immediate family unit.

Importance of the church

We'll look at this in more detail in the next chapter, but it is important for you to be involved in a local church. As a Christian you are part of the people of God (Ephesians 2:11-22). You need other people in the church to help you become a mature Christian, especially teachers and shepherds who provide this kind of help (Ephesians 4:11-14).

Church is important for you because you will hear teaching about the Lord, how to think truthfully, and how to live. This teaching should help you be able to grow spiritually in your situation. For example, if you are taught by others that you are justified in Christ (Romans 5:1), are no longer condemned because you are in him (Romans 8:1), and that no condemnation or charge against you will stand (Romans 8:33, 34), you will be better able to reject accusatory and condemning words from your husband. While it is essential that you have contact with other believers, it is important that you talk to your church leadership if your husband is trying to control who you see. They can support you and give you advice about what to do in your situation.

Having other people in your life who can teach you how to deal with any negative thoughts you may have, such as being a failure or a bad wife, will help you live as the Bible teaches rather than come under the control of your husband. Being in relationship with other people will also prevent isolation, which will help stop your husband controlling you. This is especially true if there are people in the church who know about your situation, who believe you and in you, and do not take his good behavior in public at face value.

Debbie's story

Debbie now understood that her purpose in life is to live for the glory of Christ and not to live for her husband. By living for the glory of Christ she could relate differently to Pete. For the first time she came to see that if he would ask her to sin, or do or say something that would prevent her from living for the glory of God (or something that made it easier for him to sin against her) she should refuse to submit. In areas which are not specifically mentioned in Scripture, she would need wisdom to know where being submissive to him would lead to. If it leads to him having control over her, it would be wise to put boundaries in place because nobody should be allowed to have control over her.

Debbie also understood how she could change. This comes about as she lets the Lord work on her heart, (her moral core) to conform to Christ. Instead of living in confusion and doubt, worry, fear, guilt, anger, shame, loneliness, and/ or depression, she can live for the glory of Christ. In the home, she can learn to respond to Pete's abusive speech by responding in a calm and loving way while confronting him about his sin. She could set boundaries to prevent him from being able to sin against her, and so that she is able to freely follow the Lord. A local church and friendship with other believers are important for her as they help her mature in the Lord, they help to counter any falsehoods Pete may be teaching her, and help bring her out of isolation.

Questions for Reflection

1. Read Romans 6:12-15; Colossians 1:21 22; Ephesians 1:4; Romans 8:29; and 1 Peter 1:2. What do each of these verses call you to do? As you think about your marriage, in what way will practicing this affect how you think about and relate to your husband?

2. Read Ephesians 1 and take note of all that God the Father, Son, and Spirit have done. According to the passage, what does that mean for you? Think about and write down the way these truths impact how you see yourself and how you relate to other people, especially your husband. When you become upset, or you have choices that you need to make, what role does the Lord play in these choices? What role does your husband play? When you are upset keep a record of the things that you think about yourself. Examine these thoughts in the light of what the Bible says about who you are as a believer. Actively consider these biblical truths instead of what comes out of your own heart or other people's judgments about you. It is also helpful to speak Bible verses or

passages out loud since this helps us fill our minds with these truths.

3. When your husband is trying to get you to do something, keep a record of how you respond to him. Are these responses part of what belongs to the old nature? Read Galatians 5:19-21; Colossians 3:5-10; Ephesians 4:20-32; Romans 1: 28-32; and Mark 7:21-23 to help you. When your husband puts pressure on you, is he treating you according to what is of the old nature? Read Romans 6 and 8, and then go back to Romans 8:12, 13. Instead of going along with thinking and behavior consistent with the old nature, how are you to respond?

4. Can you give a short definition of the 'heart' in Scripture?

5. Keep a 'thought' journal, a record of your thoughts. If your husband accuses you, exaggerates, insinuates, twists facts, or tries to make you feel guilty, write down what it is that he says to you. What did you think in response? Are these in agreement with what the Bible says about you as someone who is created, fallen, and now redeemed?

6. Mind – you are called to glorify the Lord with your mind. This means thinking God-honoring truthful thoughts. Use your thought journal to see what patterns of thinking you have. Read Ephesians 4:20-24. Since you are called to be renewed in the spirit of your mind (i.e. the attitude of your mind, your way of thinking), examine Scripture to see what it says about the thoughts that you have listed, then consciously choose to think and focus on what is true. Having Bible verses with you or near you in places where you go regularly can be a tremendous help for turning your thoughts away from what is not of the Lord (and therefore not helpful) to what is truthful. For example, I write out helpful Bible verses on cards or type them in my phone, when I have to be in situations that I find difficult.

Keep truths in mind that will help you focus on knowing the Lord when you are relating to your husband. Take a note of when your main motive becomes pleasing your husband and/or trying to change his behavior.

List the times when you tend to doubt your ability to perceive and understand reality. It is essential for you to be live in what is true and according to the truth. Bring your focus back to honoring Jesus by thinking about biblical truth and speaking it out loud. If necessary ask a trusted friend who understands your situation about the situation that is confusing you. Remember that your motive is to live and think in ways that please God.

7. Worry – In your thought journal, what do you see are the things that you worry about? Read Matthew 6:19-36. As you trust God, what does he promise you? Write down how God has cared for you in the past. He promises to care for you throughout your life.

Read the following attributes of God:

- Omnipresent – he is everywhere (Jeremiah 23:23-24; Psalm 139:7-10)

- Omniscient – he knows everything (1 John 3:20; Psalm 139:1-2, 4, 16)
- Wise (Romans 16:27; 1 Corinthians 1:24, 30; Ephesians 3:10)
- Faithful (Deuteronomy 32:4)
- Good (Luke 18:19; Psalm 100:5; Psalm 106:1; Psalm 107:1; Psalm 34:8)
- Loving (1 John 4:8; John 3:16; Galatians 2:20)
- Merciful (2 Corinthians 1:3)
- Gracious (Romans 3:24; 2 Corinthians 8:9; Ephesians 2:8)
- Holy (Psalm 71:22; 78:41; 89:18; Isaiah 1:4; 5:19, 24; 6:3; 1 Peter 1:16)
- Righteous (Deuteronomy 32:4)
- Jealous (Exodus 34:14;Deuteronomy 4:24; 5:9)
- Full of wrath (Exodus 32:9-10; Deuteronomy 9:7-8; 29:23; 2 Kings 22:13; Romans 1:18)
- Omnipotent – he is all powerful (Psalm 24:8; Genesis 18:14; Jeremiah 32:27; Revelation 1:8)
- Longsuffering / patient (Exodus 34:6; Psalm 86:15; Romans 2:4; 9:22; 1 Peter 3:20; 2 Peter 3:15)[63]

Think about how each attribute applies to the things you worry about. Be specific. When you sense that you are beginning to worry, prayerfully bring your mind back to the character of God.

8.   Guilt – According to your thought journal, what are the things that you feel guilty about? Confess any sin to the Lord. Do you feel guilty because you did not meet a standard set by your husband that is not addressed by the Bible? Examine his claim against Scripture. Read 2 Corinthians 5:21; Romans 3:24; 8:1, 30, 33, 34. If what you are being accused of is not sin, focus on this truth: in Christ there is no condemnation. Since you have been clothed with the righteousness of Christ, you can know that the Lord sees you as righteous.

If you are guilty of sin, confess this to the Lord, then read the same Bible verses as above and focus on the truth that you have been clothed with the righteousness of Christ. There are answers in the Bible for dealing with guilt. Since your guilt has been paid for and removed, you are not supposed to live in it.

9. Anger – when you get angry, what is it that you think is wrong and/or unjust?

    What angry thoughts do you have? How do you express your anger? What do you want that you do not have? As you seek to live for the glory of God, it is important to work on your heart and how you express your words and thoughts when you become angry. Speak to a trusted friend who understands your situation about how to work on the areas that lead to you becoming angry. You may need practical help from others as you do this.

10. Shame – in what ways do you think that you are inadequate? In what ways does your husband say that you fail as a person? Read Genesis 3:7 and 3:21. What did God do with Adam and Eve's shame? Read Isaiah 53:3-5. In what way did Jesus experience shame? Read Isaiah 54:4-6. In what way were the people of Israel to deal with their shame? Read Hebrews 12:1, 2. How did Jesus deal with the shame of the cross? Where was his focus? Read 2 Corinthians 5:21; Romans 5:1; 8:1; and Ephesians 1:4. What truths about yourself do you see in these verses?

11. Loneliness – Read Psalm 139:7-12; Isaiah 41:10; Matthew 28:20; and Hebrews 13:5. What does the Lord promise you? As a believer and member of the body of Christ, it is important that you have fellowship with other believers. Think about how you can build friendships with a few godly women. Be wise and careful as coming out of your isolation will probably upset your husband.

12. Depression – It is important to keep a daily and weekly schedule as you live for the glory of the God and let him work on your heart. Decide at what time you will get up in the morning and go to bed at night. Plan in time for exercise. Make a list of all the responsibilities you have (with the help of a trusted friend if necessary) and make a weekly schedule that is realistic and achievable.

13. Home – Re-read the section in the chapter about speech. How do you normally respond to your husband's attacking speech? Think through ways in which you can respond that are good and honor the Lord. You may want to ask a friend to help you do this.

5. Church Involvement

Erika's lifeline was the church. When she started to change, her husband David wasn't pleased. He went into overdrive, using all the techniques that had worked to get her under his control in the past. Some people in the church saw what was happening and provided practical and spiritual support. They babysat, helped get legal advice, ensured she could work, and approached David in a wise way. Knowing that the most loving thing for David was to help him live in a different way, they did all they could to help him change and kept him accountable for how he treated Erika and their children.

What is the church?

In the Scriptures we read that God called people to have a special relationship with him. This began with the calling of Abraham in Genesis 12:1-3. God promised to bless Abraham and to make him into a great nation, and promised that his descendants would inherit the land of Canaan (Genesis 17:1-8). The people of Israel are God's people who descended from their forefather Abraham.

In the New Testament, 'God's people' is expanded beyond the people of Israel to also include people from other nations through faith in Christ (1 Peter 2:10). Both Jewish and non-Jewish believers are equal in him (Galatians 3:28). God's people, the Church, consists of people from different nationalities who are in Christ.

Various images are used of the Church in the New Testament:

- God's family (1 Timothy 5:1-2; 2 Corinthians 6:18; Matthew 12:49-50; and 1 John 3:14-18)
- The bride of Christ (Ephesians 5:32; 2 Corinthians 11:2)
- Branches of a vine (John 15:5)
- An olive tree (Romans 11:17-24)
- A field of crops (1 Corinthians 3:6-9)
- A building (1 Corinthians 3:9)
- A harvest (Matthew 13:1-30; John 4:35)
- God's house (Hebrews 3:3-6)
- The pillar and bulwark of the truth (1 Timothy 3:15)
- The body of Christ (1 Corinthians 12:12-27; Ephesians 1:22-23; 4:15-16; Colossians 1:18, 2:19)
- The temple of God, or the city Jerusalem above (Galatians 4:26; Hebrews 12:22; Revelation 21:2)

The church as the body of Christ

As the body of Christ, all believers are united with one another in relationship. Believers are united together as members of the body of Jesus Christ, who is the Head of the body and nourishes, feeds, and rules it (Colossians 1:18).

Each member has been given spiritual gifts to be used to edify and to strengthen others for the common good (1 Corinthians 12:4-31). It is through the use of spiritual gifts that others can walk with you and help you fulfil your calling in life. Some spiritual gifts are of special importance. For example, those gifted with words of wisdom (1 Corinthians 12:8) can help you with advice about how to live in your particular situation. Teaching is needed in order to know the Lord and how to live in a way that he desires. Exhortation can help you persevere in living God's way. Mercy is important for when you experience a particular difficulty or have made mistakes or sinned in response to something your husband has said or done (Romans 12:8).

The church as the temple of God

The church is called the temple of God (1 Corinthians 3:16; Ephesians 2:21, 22; 1 Peter 2:5). The Lord indwells it, and it is therefore holy. As members of God's temple, believers are called to live holy lives (1 Corinthians 6:19-20). Being part of the temple of God means that you will live in a different way than your husband, since he is not living in the same holy way as you are seeking to do. By becoming holy you will *not* be the person that he wants you to be. You will probably need the help and support of other believers as you seek to continue living in this way.

The church as the pillar and buttress of the truth

As the pillar and buttress of the truth, the church is to guard the truth and defend it against its enemies (1 Timothy 3:15).[64] This involves preventing wrong teaching (1 Timothy 1:3, 4; Titus 1:9-11). In a good church you can hear teaching about what marriage is and how husbands and wives are to relate to each other. Teaching about justification will help you know how to deal with guilt and that it is impossible to live to meet other people's expectations.

The church as the people of God

As the people of God (2 Corinthians 6:16) the church belongs to God. As a believer, you belong to God in the first place. Being a member of the people of God includes living in a way that honors and glorifies the Lord, which will be expressed in how you relate to your husband.

The church as a priesthood

All believers are priests (1 Peter 2:9; Hebrews 13:15-16). You can ask other believers to intercede for you before the Lord so that you will continue and persevere in living a God-honoring life, and that the Holy Spirit will work on your husband's heart so that he becomes aware of his wrongdoing and comes to a place of godly repentance (2 Corinthians 7:10).

Relating to one another

Many passages in Scripture speak about the role that believers have with each another. For example believers are to instruct one another (Romans 15:14), teach and admonish one another in all wisdom (Colossians 3:16), and encourage and build one another up (1 Thessalonians 5:11; Ephesians 4:12, 29). Believers are to consider how to spur each other toward love and good works (Hebrews 10:24-25). Try to become involved in the life of a few women who can encourage and instruct you in your situation.

The church as the family of God

Church members are intimately connected to each other as members of the family of God. Paul taught Timothy that he was to encourage older men as fathers, younger men as brothers, older women as mothers, and younger women as sisters (1 Timothy 5:1, 2). God is the heavenly father of all believers (Ephesians 3:14, 15; 2 Corinthians 6:18). As the family of God there should be love and fellowship between members of a local church and you. Try to find some older women who can teach you practically how to be a godly woman (Titus 2:3-5).

Your whole family will need support from the leadership of the church. Christian love for your husband is expressed by them by talking to him about the way that he treats you and your children. They are loving him by helping him change and doing all they can to support your family and to prevent him from treating you in abusive ways.

The church community should be a place where it is known that abuse, manipulation, and control will not be tolerated, and that anybody who behaves in this way will be helped to change. It is important for the church to become aware of the legal issues involved in abuse situations. For example, they should know what the legal rights of the children are, what financial responsibilities each partner has, what the legal ramifications are if one spouse leaves the home, and what they can and cannot do as a church.

Caring for the weak

Believers are called to care for the weak in society. In the Old Testament God's people were called to care for the fatherless, the widow, and foreigners, just as the Lord cared for them (Deuteronomy 10:17-19). In biblical times, widows and orphans had no male figure to provide for them, which meant that they were in an especially vulnerable position. We see this when Jesus raised a widow's son from the dead (Luke 7:11-17). Since she had no husband or son to provide for her, the widow had no means of survival. Believers in the New Testament are to care for orphans and widows (James 1:27) and to provide for those who need clothing and food (James 2:14-17; 1 John 3:16-18).

If your husband does not provide enough finances for your family, speak to someone in your church leadership you trust. Ask them for help and advice about how to care for yourself and your children without having to give in to your husband's control in order to do so. Please be sure to ask this as part of the help the church is giving you so that the advice given is part of the big picture of what is going on in your situation.

Debbie's story

The supportive church

Debbie understood the importance of church. She wanted to get wise help for her church family and didn't want to disrespect or malign her husband in any way. Pete was highly respected in their local church. Debbie prayerfully considered which women she would spend time with and confide in so that she would find help to live in the truth and have other women speaking into her life. She went to Ian, an elder she trusted, explaining her situation and asking for help for all of her family. Having known Pete and Debbie for many years, Ian knew he could carefully approach Pete. He also knew that he had to do it wisely so that it did not result in further suffering for Debbie. Over a period of months, Ian worked with Pete to help him repent of his domineering control and to lovingly care for his wife and children. Ian made sure that Debbie and the kids were protected, had enough financial income, and that Debbie could spend time with other women in the church who helped her live in a God-honoring way. Ian was thankful for the way that things were working out, but he had heard plenty stories of abusive men who changed only for as long as pressure was put on them. He knew he had to support this family for many years. He also knew abusive people seldom change. He was thankful for what he saw, while he continued to pray for genuine lasting repentance and change.

Closing Thoughts

BY READING THIS book I hope you have come to see that you can know the Lord and become like him. You will have read that this change is active. What I have written about is incredibly difficult and is usually responded to with hostility: your husband will not like it. I can't promise you that he will change. While I can't promise you this, I have seen the Lord take abusive men and slowly turn them to become godly men. Support from wise and understanding friends and church leaders is essential. I have worked with abused women for decades and have seen the Lord change countless lives. Remember, God is *for* and *with* you.

Bibliography

Note: _____ . means same author as the one immediately before.

Achtemeier, Paul. *Romans. Interpretation. A Bible Commentary for Teaching and Preaching.* Louisville: John Knox Press, 1985.

Adams, Jay. *Handbook of Church Discipline: A Right and Privilege of Every Church Member.* Grand Rapids: Zondervan, 1974.

_____. *Language of Counseling.* Stanley: Timeless Texts, 1981.

American Association of Christian Counselors. "Mission," http://www.aacc.net/about-us/ (accessed April 6, 2015).

Amos, Clare. *The Book of Genesis.* Werrington: Biddles Ltd., 2004.

Antai,Diddy. "Controlling behavior, power relations within intimate relationships and intimate partner physical and sexual violence against women in Nigeria."

BMC Public Health 11:511(2011). http://www.biomedcentral.com/1471-2458/11/511 (accessed November 10, 2014).

Arnold, Bill. *Genesis. The New Cambridge Bible Commentary.* New York: Cambridge University Press, 2009.

Balswick, Judith and Jack Balswick. "Marriage as a Partnership of Equals." In *Discovering Biblical Equality: Complementarity Without Hierarchy.* edited by Ronald Pierce and Rebecca Groothuis448-463. Downers Grove: Inter-varsity Press, 2005.

Belleville, Linda. "Women in Ministry: An Egalitarian Perspective." In *Two Views on Women in Ministry,* edited by James Beck and Linda Belleville, 19-119. Grand Rapids: Zondervan, 2005.

_____. *Women Leaders and the Church.* Grand Rapids: Baker Books, 2000.

Berkhof, Louis. *Systematic Theology.*15th ed. Edinburgh: The Banner of Truth Trust, 2000.

Blomberg, Craig. *1 Corinthians. The NIV Application Commentary.* Grand Rapids: Zondervan Publishing House, 1994.

_____. "Women in Ministry: A Complementarian Perspective." In *Two Views on Women in Ministry,* edited by James Beck and Linda Belleville 123-184. Grand Rapids: Zondervan, 2005.

Bordwine, James. *The Pauline Doctrine of Male*

Headship. The Apostle versus Biblical Feminists.
Greenville: Greenville Seminary Press, 1996.

Briscoe, D. *The Preacher's Commentary: Genesis*
Nashville: Thomas Nelson Publishers, 1987.

Bruce, F.F. *The Epistle to the Colossians to Philemon
and to the Ephesians.* Grand Rapids: Wm. Eerdmans
Publishing Co., 1984.

_____. *The Epistle to the Ephesians.* London: Pickering
&Inglis, Ltd., 1961.

Brueggeman, Walter. *Genesis. A Bible Commentary
for Teaching and Preaching.* Atlanta: John Knox Press,
1982.

Cloud, Henry, & John Townsend. *Boundaries: When
to Say Yes. When to Say No to Take Control of Your Life.*
Grand Rapids: Zondervan, 1992.

Davids, Peter. *Ephesians, Philippians, Colossians,
1-2 Thessalonians, Philemon. Cornerstone Biblical
Commentary.* Edited by Philip Comfort. Carol Stream:
Tyndale House Publishers, 2008.

_____. "A Silent Witness in Marriage: 1 Peter 3:1-7."
In *Discovering Biblical Equality: Complementarity
Without Hierarchy.* edited by Ronald Pierce and
Rebecca Groothuis, 224-238. Downers Grove: Inter-
varsity Press, 2005.

Davidson, R. *Genesis 1-11. The Cambridge Bible
Commentary on the New English Bible.* Cambridge
University Press, 1973.

Ellis, Albert, and Marcia Powers. *The Secret of Overcoming Verbal Abuse: Getting Off the Emotional Roller Coaster and Regaining Control of Your Life.* Hollywood: Wilshire Book Company, 2000.

Engel, Beverly. *The Emotionally Abused Woman: Overcoming Destructive Patterns and Reclaiming Yourself.* New York: Fawcett Books, 1990.

_____. *The Emotionally Abusive Relationship: How to Stop Being Abused and How to Stop Abusing.* Hoboken: John Wiley & Sons Inc., 2002.

Erickson, Millard. *Christian Theology.* 13th ed. Grand Rapids: Baker Book House, 1985.

Evans, Patricia. *The Verbally Abusive Relationship: How to Recognize it and How to Respond.* Avon, MA: Adams Media, 2010.

Eyrich, Howard and William Hines. *Curing the Heart: A Model for Biblical Counseling.* Fearn: Christian Focus Publications Ltd., 2002.

Fitzpatrick, Elyse. "Christ's Word to Worriers." *Institute for Counseling and Discipleship.* Summer Institute 2011, mp3.

_____. *Helper by Design: God's Perfect Plan for Women in Marriage.* Chicago: Moody Publishers, 2003.

Follingstad, Diane and Dana Dehart. "Defining Psychological Abuse of Husbands Toward Wives Contexts, Behaviors, and Typologies." *Journal of*

Interpersonal Violence 15, no. 9 (September 2000): 891-920.

Frame, John. "Men and Women in the Image of God," In *Recovering Biblical Manhood and Womanhood,* edited by John Piper and Wayne Grudem, 228-236. Wheaton: Crossway Books, 1991.

Gaebelein, Frank. *The Expositor's Bible Commentary. Genesis, Exodus, Leviticus, Numbers.* Grand Rapids: Zondervan Publishing House, 1990.

Galloway, Sid. "Wife Abuse." *National Association of Nouthetic Counselors.* Annual Conference 1992. CD N9209.

Gispen, W. *Commentaar op het Oude Testament: Genesis 1-11.* Kampen: J.H. Kok, 1974.

Goode, Wm. "Wife Abuse (90)." *National Association of Nouthetic Counselors.* Annual Conference 1990. CD N9027.

Groothuis, Rebecca. "Equal in Being, Unequal in Role: Exploring the Logic of Women's Subordination." In *Discovering Biblical Equality: Complementarity Without Hierarchy,* edited by Ronald Pierce and Rebecca Groothuis, 301-333. Downers Grove: Inter-varsity Press, 2005.

Grudem, Wayne. "The Key Issues in the Manhood and Womanhood Controversy, And The Way Forward." In *Biblical Foundations for Manhood and Womanhood,* edited by Wayne Grudem, 19-68.Wheaton: Crossway Books, 2002.

_____. *Systematic Theology: An Introduction to Biblical Doctrine.* Leicester: Inter-varsity Press, 1994.

Hay, David. *Colossians.* Nashville: Abingdon Press, 2000.

Hendrickson, Laura. "Counseling Victims of Spousal Abuse." *Institute for Biblical Counseling & Discipleship.* mp3. http://www.ibcd.org/resources/messages/counseling-victims-of-spousal-abuse/ (accessed January 16, 2014).

Hendrikson, William. *New Testament Commentary: Exposition of Colossians and Philemon.* Grand Rapids: Baker Book House, 1975.

Hess, Richard. "Equality With and Without Innocence: Genesis 1-3." In *Discovering Biblical Equality: Complementarity Without Hierarchy,* edited by Ronald Pierce and Rebecca Groothuis, 481-493. Downers Grove: Inter-varsity Press, 2005.

Hirigoyen, Marie-France. *Stalking the Soul: Emotional Abuse and the Erosion of Identity.* New York: Helen Marx Books, 2004.

Holcomb Justin and Lindsay Holcomb. *Rid of My Disgrace: Hope and Healing for Victims of Sexual Assault.* Wheaton: Crossway, 2011.

Horsley, Richard. *1 Corinthians.* Nashville: Abingdon Press, 1998.

Hunt, June. *How to Rise Above Abuse: Victory for Victims of Five Types of Abuse.* Eugene: Harvest House Publishers, 2010.

Hurley, James. *Man and Women in Biblical Perspective.* Leicester: Inter-varsity Press, 2005.

Jackson, Tim. "Emotionally Destructive Marriages." *RBC Webinars,* May 3rd 2014. http://helpformylife.org/2014/03/05/the-emotionally-destructive-marriage-webinar (accessed July 13, 2014).

Kelleman, Robert. "Counseling and Abuse in Marriage." *RPM Ministries.* Pdf.

_____. *Sexual Abuse: Beauty for Ashes.* Phillipsburg: P&R Publishing, 2013.

Kimball, Cynthia. "Nature, Culture, and Gender Complementarity," In *Discovering Biblical Equality: Complementarity Without Hierarchy,* edited by Ronald Pierce and Rebecca Groothuis464-480. Downers Grove: Inter-varsity Press, 2005.

Kistemaker, Simon. *1 Corinthians. New Testament Commentary.* Grand Rapids: Zondervan Publishing House, 1994.

Knight, George. "The Family and the Church: How Should Biblical Manhood and Womanhood Work Out in Practice?" In *Recovering Biblical Manhood and Womanhood,* edited by John Piper and Wayne Grudem, 161-175.Wheaton: Crossway Books, 1991.

_____. "Husbands and Wives as Analogies of Christ

and the Church. Ephesians 5:21-33 and Colossians 3:18-19." In *Recovering Biblical Manhood and Womanhood.* edited by John Piper and Wayne Grudem, 161-175.Wheaton: Crossway Books, 1991.

Liefield, Walter. "The Nature of Authority in the New Testament." In *Discovering Biblical Equality: Complementarity Without Hierarchy,* edited by Ronald Pierce and Rebecca Groothuis, 255-271. Downers Grove: Inter-varsity Press, 2005.

Loring, Marti. *Emotional Abuse.* San Francisco: Jossey-Bass Publishers, 1994.

MacArthur, John. *Galatians.* Chicago: The Moody Press, 1987.

Mack, Wayne. "Biblical Help for Overcoming Despondency, Depression." *The Journal of Pastoral Practice* II, no. 2. (1978): 31-48.

_____. "Loneliness & Self-Pity#1: How to Handle Loneliness." *The Dr. Wayne Mack Library.* CDWM4191.

Marshall, I. "Mutual Love and Submission in Marriage. Colossians 3:18-19 and Ephesians 5:21-33." In *Discovering Biblical Equality: Complementarity Without Hierarchy,* edited by Ronald Pierce and Rebecca Groothuis, 186-204. Downers Grove: Inter-varsity Press, 2005.

Matteus, Kenneth. *Genesis 1-11: 26. Vol 1A. An Exegetical & Theological Exposition Holy Scripture.*

The New American Commentary. Nashville: B&H Publishing Group, 1996.

Mercadante, Linda. *From Hierarchy to Equality: A Comparison of Past and Present Interpretations of 1 Corinthians 11:2-16 in Relation to the Changing Status of Women in Society.* Vancouver: Regent College, 1978.

Miller, Mary. *No Visible Wounds: Identifying Nonphysical Abuse of Women by their Men.* New York: Ballantine Books, 1995.

Mounce, Robert. *Romans. The New American Commentary. An Exegetical and Theological Exposition of Holy Scripture* (Nashville: Broadman and Holman Publishers, 1995), 149.

Needham, Robert. "Abuse: Addressing It." *Institute for Biblical Counseling & Discipleship.* mp3. February 10th, 2013. http://ibcd.org/resources/messages/cdc1-14-1angerabuse/ (accessed January 16, 2014).

_____. "Abuse: Recognizing It." *Institute for Biblical Counseling & Discipleship.* mp3. http://www.soundword.com/ab1reitm.html (accessed January 16, 2014).

Neuer, Werner. *Man & Woman in Christian Perspective.* London: Hodder & Stoughton, 1990.

Newheiser, Jim. "Anger/Abuse." *Institute for Biblical Counseling & Discipleship,* mp3, February 10th, 2013. http://www.ibcd.org/resources/messages/cdc1-14-angerabuse/ (accessed January 16, 2014).

_____. "Church Discipline: 1 Corinthians 5." *Institute for Biblical Counseling & Discipleship.* mp3.

Newheiser, Caroline. "Helping Women who are Married but Lonely." *The Institute for Biblical Counseling and Discipleship.* Summer Institute 2013. mp3.

NiCarthy, Ginny. *Getting Free: A Handbook for Women in Abusive Situations.* Worcester: Billing & Sons, Ltd., 1991).

Nicole, Roger. "Biblical Hermeneutics: Basic Principles and Questions of Gender." In *Discovering Biblical Equality: Complementarity Without Hierarchy,* edited by Ronald Pierce and Rebecca Groothuis, 355-363. Downers Grove: Inter-varsity Press, 2005.

Nicols, Brittney. "Violence Against Women: The Extent of the Problem." In *"Intimate Violence Against Women: When Spouses, Partners, or Lovers Attack.* edited by Paula Lundberg-Love and Shelly Marmion, 1-8. Westport: Praeger Publishers, 2006.

Novsak, Rachel., Tina Mandelj, and Barbara Simonic. "Therapeutic Implications of Religious-Related Emotional Abuse." *Journal of Aggression, Maltreatment, & Trauma* Vol. 21, Issue 1 (2012): 31-44.

O'Brien, Peter. *Colossians, Philemon. Word Biblical Commentary.* Waco: Word Books, 1982.

_____. *The Letter to the Ephesians. Pillar The New Testament Commentary* (Leicester: Apollos, 1999.

Ortland, Raymond. "Male-Female Equality and Headship: Genesis 1-3." In *Recovering Biblical Manhood and Womanhood,* edited by John Piper and Wayne Grudem, 86-104. Wheaton: Crossway Books, 1991.

Osbourne, Grant. ed. *Romans. The I.V.P. New Testament Commentary Series.* Downers Grove: Intervarsity Press, 2004.

Oxford Concise English Dictionary of Current English 9th ed.(New York: Oxford University Press, 1995.

Patzia, Arthur. *Ephesians, Colossians, Philemon. New International Biblical Commentary.* Peabody: Hendrickson, 1990.

Pieters, Jerome et al. "Emotional, Physical, and Sexual Abuse: The Experiences of Men and Women." *Institute for the Equality of Men and Women.* http ://igvm-iefh. belgium.be. (Accessed November 10, 2014).

Piper, John. "An Overview of Critical Concerns: Questions and Answers." In *Recovering Biblical Manhood and Womanhood,* edited by John Piper and Wayne Grudem, 25-55. Wheaton: Crossway Books, 1991.

_____. "A Vision of Biblical Complementarity: Manhood and Womanhood Defined According to the Bible." In *Recovering Biblical Manhood and Womanhood,* edited by John Piper and Wayne Grudem, 25-55. Wheaton: Crossway Books, 1991.

Powlison, David. "The River of Life Flows Through the

Slough of Despond." *The Journal of Biblical Counseling,* 18, no. 2 (Winter 2000), 2-4.

Priolo, Lou. "Biblical Resources for the Wife's Protection." *The Lou Priolo Audio Library.* CD LP40.

_____. "Counseling Angry People." *The Institute for Biblical Counseling & Discipleship,* mp3, June 26th, 2008. http://www.ibcd.org/resources/messages/counseling-angry-people/ (accessed January 17, 2014).

_____. "Helping People Pleasers." *National Association of Nouthetic Counselors.* Conference 2006. mp3.

_____. "How to Respond to Rejection and Hurt." *The Lou Priolo Library.* CD LP52b.

Pryde, Debi, & Robert Needham. *A Biblical Perspective of What to Do When You are Abused by Your Husband.* New Springs: Iron Sharpeneth Iron Publications, 2003.

Rinck, Margaret. *Christian Men who Hate Women.* Grand Rapids: Zondervan, 1990.

Ross, Allen. *Genesis. Cornerstone Biblical Commentary.* Carol Stream, Illinois: Tyndale House Publishers, 2008.

Ryken, Leland, James Wilhoit, and Tremper Longman. ed. *Dictionary of Biblical Imagery: An encyclopedic exploration of the images, symbols, motifs, metaphors, figures of speech and literary patterns of the Bible.* Downers Grove: InterVarsity Press USA.

Ryken, Philip. *Galatians. Reformed Expository Commentary.* Phillipsburg: P&R Publishing, 2005.

Sande, Ken. "Redemptive Church Discipline." *Institute for Biblical Counseling & Discipleship.* Summer Institute. 2009. mp3.

Scheckter, Sarah. "Emotionally Abusive Relationships." *Perelman School of Medicine, Department of Psychiatry Penn Behavioral Health* http://www.med.upenn.edu/psychotherapy/Schechter--EmotionallyAbusive.html (accessed January 8, 2014).

Schreiner, Thomas. "Women in Ministry: Another Complementarian Perspective." In *Two Views on Women in Ministry,* edited by James Beck and Linda Belleville, 265-342. Grand Rapids: Zondervan, 2005.

Scipione, George. "How to Counsel Spousal Abuse." *National Association of Nouthetic Counselors.* Conference 1999. CD N9938.

_____. "Worry." *CCEF – West San Diego 92.* CD ibc9233.

Somerville, Mary. "Coping with Loneliness." *National Association of Nouthetic Counselors*, Annual Conference, 2005, mp3.

Spencer, Aida. "Jesus' Treatment of Women in the Gospels." In *Discovering Biblical Equality: Complementarity Without Hierarchy,* edited by Ronald Pierce and Rebecca Groothuis, 126-141. Downers Grove: Inter-varsity Press, 2005.

Stark, Evan. *Coercive Control: How Men Entrap Women*

in Personal Life. New York: Oxford University Press, 2007.

Storkey, Elaine. *Created or Constructed: The Great Gender Debate.* Carlisle: Paternoster Press, 2000.

Stott, John. *The Message of Galatians. The Bible Speaks Today.* Leicester: Inter-Varsity Press, 1968.

_____. *The Message of 1 Timothy & Titus: The Bible Speaks Today.* Leicester: Inter-varsity Press, 1996.

Street, John. "Handle with Care: Counseling Abuse Victims." *National Association of Nouthetic Counselors* Conference 2012, mp3.

The Biblical Counseling Coalition. "Confessional Statement." http://biblicalcounselingcoalition.org/about/confessional-statement/ (accessed May 31, 2014).

Tracy, Steven. *Mending the Soul: Understanding and Healing Abuse.* Grand Rapids: Zondervan, 2005.

United Nations. "International Day for the Elimination of Violence Against Women." http://www.un.org/en/events/endviolenceday/ (accessed May 31, 2014).

Uprichard, Richard. *Ephesians. An EP Commentary.* Auburn: Evangelical Press, 2004.

Vernick, Leslie. *The Emotionally Destructive Marriage.* Colorado Springs: WaterBrook Press, 2013.

_____. *How to Act Right When Your Spouse Acts Wrong.* Colorado Springs: WaterBrook Press, 2001.

Wall, Robert. *Colossians and Philemon. The IVP New Testament Commentary Series.* Downers Grove: Intervarsity Press, 1993.

Ware, Bruce. "Male and Female Complementarity and the Image of God." In *Biblical Foundations for Manhood and Womanhood,* edited by Wayne Grudem,71-92. Wheaton: Crossway Books, 2002.

Welch, Ed. *Blame it on the Brain: Distinguishing Chemical Imbalances, Brain Disorders, and Disobedience.* Phillipsburg: P&R Publishing, 1998.

_____. "Boundaries in Relationships," *The Journal of Biblical Counseling* 23, no. 3 (January 2004):15-24.

_____. "Counseling Those Who Are Depressed," *The Journal of Biblical Counseling* 18, no. 2 (Winter 2000):5-7.

_____. *Depression: Looking Up from the Stubborn Darkness.* Greensboro: New Growth Press, 2011.

_____. "Helping Those Who Are Depressed." *The Journal of Biblical Counseling* 18, no. 2 (Winter 2000): 25-31.

_____. *Shame Interrupted: How God Lifts the Pain of Worthlessness & Rejection* Greensboro: New Growth Press, 2012.

_____. "Understanding Depression." *The Journal of Biblical Counseling* 18, no. 2 (Winter 2000): 12-24.

_____. *When People are Big and God is Small:*

Overcoming Peer Pressure, Codependency, and the Fear of Man. Phillipsburg: P&R Publishing, 1997.

_____. "Words of Hope for Those Who Struggle with Depression." *The Journal of Biblical Counseling* 18, no. 2 (Winter 2000): 40-46.

Wenham, Gordon. *Genesis 1-15. Word Biblical Commentary.* Waco: Word Books Publishers, 1987.

Westwood, Tom. *Colossians.* Redlands: Bible Treasury Hour Inc., 1970.

Wright, R. "God, Metaphor and Gender: Is the God of the Bible a Male Deity?" In *Discovering Biblical Equality: Complementarity Without Hierarchy,* edited by Ronald Pierce and Rebecca Groothuis287-300. Downers Grove: Intervarsity Press, 2005.

Endnotes

Note: _____. means same author as the one immediately before.

1   This definition is an expansion of Engel's definition in Beverly Engel, The Emotionally Abusive Relationship: How to Stop Being Abused and How to Stop Abusing (Hoboken: John Wiley & Sons Inc., 2002), 10. This definition includes the effect of emotional abuse on the victim.

2   Loring, Emotional Abuse, 3; Nicols, "Violence Against Women: The Extent of the Problem," In "Intimate Violence Against Women: When Spouses, Partners, or Lovers Attack, edited by Paula Lundberg-Love and Shelly Marmion, 16-17; Albert Ellis and Marcia Powers, The Secret of Overcoming Verbal Abuse: Getting Off the Emotional Roller Coaster and Regaining Control of Your Life (Hollywood: Wilshire Book Company, 2000), 18; Lundy Bancroft, Why Does he Do That?: Inside the Minds of Angry and Controlling Men (New York: Berkley Books, 2002), 144-145; Evans, The Verbally Abusive Relationship: How to Recognize it and How to Respond, 95; Engel,

The Emotionally Abused Woman: Overcoming Destructive Patterns and Reclaiming Yourself, 47.

3 Loring, Emotional Abuse, 3; Nicols, "Violence Against Women: The Extent of the Problem," In "Intimate Violence Against Women: When Spouses, Partners, or Lovers Attack, edited by Paula Lundberg-Love and Shelly Marmion, 17-18; Ellis and Powers, The Secret of Overcoming Verbal Abuse: Getting Off the Emotional Roller Coaster and Regaining Control of Your Life, 16-18; Engel, The Emotionally Abused Woman: Overcoming Destructive Patterns and Reclaiming Yourself, 23; Marie-France Hirigoyen, Stalking the Soul: Emotional Abuse and the Erosion of Identity (New York: Helen Marx Books, 2004), 100.

4 Stark, Coercive Control: How Men Entrap Women in Personal Life, 249.

5 Ellis and Powers, The Secret of Overcoming Verbal Abuse: Getting Off the Emotional Roller Coaster and Regaining Control of Your Life, 18.

6 Bancroft, Why Does he Do That?: Inside the Minds of Angry and Controlling Men, 125.

7 Loring, Emotional Abuse, 39.

8 _____., Emotional Abuse, 233.

9 Ellis and Powers, The Secret of Overcoming Verbal Abuse: Getting Off the Emotional Roller Coaster

and Regaining Control of Your Life, 28;Loring, Emotional Abuse, 218; Evans, The Verbally Abusive Relationship: How to Recognize it and How to Respond, 73; Hirigoyen, Stalking the Soul: Emotional Abuse and the Erosion of Identity, 155; Miller, No Visible Wounds: Identifying Nonphysical Abuse of Women by their Men, 44; Jerome Pieters et al., "Emotional, Physical, and Sexual Abuse: The Experiences of Men and Women," Institute for the Equality of Men and Women, http ://igvm-iefh.belgium.be. (Accessed November 10, 2014).

10   Belleville, Women Leaders and the Church, 100; Wayne Grudem, "The Key Issues in the Manhood and Womanhood Controversy, And The Way Forward." In Biblical Foundations for Manhood and Womanhood, ed. Wayne Grudem (Wheaton: Crossway Books, 2002), 19; James Hurley, Man and Women in Biblical Perspective (Leicester: Inter-varsity Press, 2005), 31; George Knight, "The Family and the Church: How Should Biblical Manhood and Womanhood Work Out in Practice?" In Recovering Biblical Manhood and Womanhood, ed. John Piper and Wayne Grudem (Wheaton: Crossway Books, 1991), 353; Belleville, "Women in Ministry: An Egalitarian Perspective." In Two Views on Women in Ministry, 26; Elyse Fitzpatrick, Helper by Design: God's Perfect Plan for Women in Marriage (Chicago: Moody Publishers, 2003), 19.

11   Belleville, Women Leaders and the Church,
      97; Richard Hess, "Equality With and Without
      Innocence: Genesis 1-3." In Discovering Biblical
      Equality: Complementarity Without Hierarchy,
      ed. Ronald Pierce and Rebecca Groothuis
      (Downers Grove: Inter-varsity Press, 2005),
      79; Craig Blomberg, "Women in Ministry: A
      Complementarian Perspective." In Two Views on
      Women in Ministry, ed. James Beck and Linda
      Belleville (Grand Rapids: Zondervan, 2005), 128.

12   Hess, "Equality Without Innocence: Genesis 1-3,"
      In Discovery Biblical Equality: Complementarity
      Without Hierarchy, 81; Bill Arnold, Genesis.
      The New Cambridge Bible Commentary (New
      York: Cambridge University Press, 2009), 45;
      R Davidson, Genesis 1-11. The Cambridge
      Bible Commentary on the New English Bible
      (Cambridge University Press, 1973), 24; Clare
      Amos, The Book of Genesis (Werrington: Biddles
      Ltd., 2004), 11.

13   Bruce Ware, "Male and Female Complementarity
      and the Image of God." In Biblical Foundations for
      Manhood and Womanhood, ed. Wayne Grudem
      (Wheaton: Crossway Books, 2002), 83.

14   Frank Gaebelein, The Expositor's Bible
      Commentary. Genesis, Exodus, Leviticus,
      Numbers (Grand Rapids: Zondervan Publishing
      House, 1990), 38; Arnold, Genesis. The New
      Cambridge Bible Commentary, 60.

15 Belleville, Women Leaders and the Church,
    101; Grudem, "The Key Issues in the Manhood
    and Womanhood Controversy, And The Way
    Forward," 31; Belleville, "Women in Ministry: An
    Egalitarian Perspective," 27; Briscoe, The Preacher's
    Commentary. Genesis, 43; Gordon Wenham,
    Genesis 1-15. Word Biblical Commentary
    (Waco: Word Books Publishers, 1987), 68;
    Kenneth Matteus, Genesis 1-15. Word Biblical
    Commentary, 214.

16 Oxford Concise English Dictionary of Current
    English 9th ed. (New York: Oxford University
    Press, 1995), 631.

17 Wenham, Genesis 1-15. Word Biblical
    Commentary, 68.

18 Matteus, Genesis 1-11: 26. Vol. 1A. An Exegetical
    & Theological Exposition of Holy Scripture. The
    New American Commentary, 214.

19 Hurley, Man and Woman in Biblical Perspective,
    173, 206; Simon Kistemaker, 1 Corinthians.
    New Testament Commentary (Grand Rapids:
    Zondervan Publishing House, 1994), 373.

20 Schreiner, "Women in Ministry: Another
    Complementarian Perspective." In Two Views on
    Women in Ministry, 124.

21 _____., 124; Hurley, Man and Woman
    in Biblical Perspective, 173; Richard Horsley, 1

Corinthians (Nashville: Abingdon Press, 1998), 155.

22   John Frame, "Men and Women in the Image of God," In Recovering Biblical Manhood and Womanhood, ed. John Piper and Wayne Grudem (Wheaton: Crossway Books, 1991), 230.

23   Belleville, Women Leaders and the Church, 108; Hess, "Equality With and Without Innocence: Genesis 1-3." In Discovering Biblical Equality: Complementarity Without Hierarchy, 91-92.

24   Belleville, Women Leaders and the Church, 105; Allen Ross, Genesis. Cornerstone Biblical Commentary (Carol Stream, Illinois: Tyndale House Publishers, 2008), 54.

25   Belleville, Women Leaders and the Church, 105; Cynthia Kimball, "Nature, Culture, and Gender Complementarity," In Discovering Biblical Equality: Complementarity Without Hierarchy, ed. Ronald Pierce and Rebecca Groothuis (Downers Grove: Inter-varsity Press, 2005), 470; Hurley, Man and Woman in Biblical Perspective, 219; Arnold, Genesis. The New Cambridge Bible Commentary, 70; Matteus, Genesis 1-11: 26. Vol. 1A. An Exegetical & Theological Exposition of Holy Scripture, 251; Walter Liefield, "The Nature of Authority in the New Testament," In Discovering Biblical Equality: Complementarity Without Hierarchy, ed. Ronald Pierce and Rebecca

Groothuis (Downers Grove: Inter-varsity Press, 2005), 93.

26   Schreiner, "Women in Ministry: Another Complementarian Perspective," In Two Views on Women in Ministry, 298; Grudem, "The Key Issues in the Manhood and Womanhood Controversy, And the Way Forward," In Recovering Biblical Manhood and Womanhood, 66.

27   Frame, "Men and Women in the Image of God," In Recovering Biblical Manhood and Womanhood, 228.

28   Peter Davids, Ephesians, Philippians, Colossians, 1-2 Thessalonians, Philemon. Cornerstone Biblical Commentary, ed. Philip Comfort (Carol Stream: Tyndale House Publishers, 2008), 291.

29   Marshall, "Mutual Love and Submission in Marriage. Colossians 3:18-19 and Ephesians 5:21-33," In Discovering Biblical Equality: Complementarity Without Hierarchy, 202.

30   Hurley, Man and Woman in Biblical Perspective, 142; George Knight, "Husbands and Wives as Analogies of Christ and the Church. Ephesians 5:21-33 and Colossians 3:18-19," In Recovering Biblical Manhood and Womanhood, ed. John Piper and Wayne Grudem (Wheaton: Crossway Books, 1991), 162; Peter O'Brien, Colossians, Philemon. Word Biblical Commentary (Waco:

Word Books, 1982), 221; Fitzpatrick, Helper By Design: God's Perfect Plan for Women in Marriage, 151.

31 Belleville, Women Leaders and the Church, 118; Knight, "Husbands and Wives as Analogies of Christ and the Church. Ephesians 5:21-33 and Colossians 3:18-19. In Recovering Biblical Manhood and Womanhood, 162; Pryde and Needham, A Biblical Perspective of What to Do When You Are Abused By Your Husband, 22.

32 Fitzpatrick, Helper By Design: God's Perfect Plan for Women in Marriage, 152.

33 Groothuis. "Equal in Being, Unequal in Role: Exploring the Logic of Women's Subordination." In Discovering Biblical Equality: Complementarity Without Hierarchy, 213; Werner Neuer, Man & Woman in Christian Perspective (London: Hodder & Stoughton, 1990), 125; James Bordwine, The Pauline Doctrine of Male Headship: The Apostle versus Biblical Feminists (Greenville: Greenville Seminary Press, 1996), 120; John Piper, "An Overview of Critical Concerns: Questions and Answers," In Recovering Biblical Manhood and Womanhood, ed. John Piper and Wayne Grudem (Wheaton: Crossway Books, 1991), 56; Knight, "Husbands and Wives as Analogies of the Church: Ephesians 5:21-33 and Colossians 3:18-19," In Recovering Biblical Manhood and Womanhood, 162; Wall, Colossians and Philemon: The IVP

New Testament Commentary Series, 157; Peter
O'Brien, The Letter to the Ephesians. Pillar The
New Testament Commentary (Leicester: Apollos,
1999), 412.

34 Groothuis, "Equal in Being, Unequal in Role:
    Exploring the Logic of Woman's Subordination,"
    In Discovering Biblical Equality: Complementarity
    Without Hierarchy, 313; Knight, "Husbands
    and Wives as Analogies of the Church: Ephesians
    5:21-33 and Colossians 3:18-19," In Recovering
    Biblical Manhood and Womanhood, 161, 165;
    O'Brien, The Letter to the Ephesians, 412, 417.

35 Belleville, Women Leaders and the Church, 119.

36 Peter Davids, "A Silent Witness in Marriage: 1
    Peter 3:1-7," In Discovering Biblical Equality:
    Complementarity Without Hierarchy, ed. Ronald
    Pierce and Rebecca Groothuis (Downers Grove:
    Inter-varsity Press, 2005), 226; Blomberg,
    "Women in Ministry: A Complementarian
    Perspective," In Two Views on Women in Ministry,
    176.

37 Belleville, Women Leaders and the Church, 199;
    Hurley, Man and Woman in Biblical Perspective,
    154.

38 Belleville, Women Leaders and the Church, 118;
    Knight, "Husbands and Wives as Analogies of
    Christ and the Church: Ephesians 5:21-33 and
    Colossians 3:18-19," In Recovering Biblical

Manhood and Womanhood, 162; O'Brien, The Letter to the Ephesians. The Pillar New Testament Commentary, 418; Fitzpatrick, Helper By Design: God's Perfect Plan for Women in Marriage, 96.

39   William Hendrikson, New Testament Commentary: Exposition of Colossians and Philemon (Grand Rapids: Baker Book House, 1975), 169; John Piper, "A Vision of Biblical Complementarity: Manhood and Womanhood Defined According to the Bible," In Recovering Biblical Manhood and Womanhood, ed. John Piper and Wayne Grudem (Wheaton: Crossway Books, 1991), 37; Piper, "An Overview of Critical Concerns: Questions and Answers," In Recovering Biblical Manhood and Womanhood, 56; Fitzpatrick, Helper by Design: God's Perfect Plan for Women in Marriage, 148.

40   Tom Westwood, Colossians (Redlands: Bible Treasury Hour Inc., 1970), 104; Wall, Colossians and Philemon. The IVP New Testament Commentary Series, 153; O'Brien, The Letter to the Ephesians. The Pillar New Testament Commentary, 411; Pryde and Needham, A Biblical Perspective of What to Do When You Are Abused By Your Husband, 27.

41   O'Brien, The Letter to the Ephesians. The Pillar New Testament Commentary, 418.

42   Bordwine, The Pauline Doctrine of Male Headship. The Apostle versus Biblical Feminists,

147; Fitzpatrick, Helper By Design: God's Perfect Plan for Women in Marriage, 148.

43 Piper, "A Vision of Biblical Complementarity: Manhood and Womanhood Defined According to the Bible," In Recovering Biblical Manhood and Womanhood, 310; Schreiner, "Women in Ministry: Another Complementarian Perspective," In Two Views on Women in Ministry, 298; Patzia, Ephesians, Colossians, 1-2 Thessalonians, Philemon. Cornerstone Biblical Commentary, 269.

44 Hurley, Man and Woman in Biblical Perspective, 142; Knight, "Husbands and Wives as Analogies of Christ and the Church: Ephesians 5:21-33 and Colossians 3:18-19," In Recovering Biblical Manhood and Womanhood, 162; O'Brien, Colossians, Philemon. Word Biblical Commentary, 221; Fitzpatrick, Helper by Design: God's Perfect Plan for Women in Marriage, 151.

45 Belleville, Women Leaders and the Church, 118; Knight, "Husbands and Wives as Analogies of Christ and the Church: Ephesians 5:21-33 and Colossians 3:18-19," In Recovering Biblical Manhood and Womanhood, 162; Pryde and Needham, A Biblical Perspective of What to Do When You Are Abused By Your Husband, 22.

46 Seeming contradictions in Scripture, especially between the Old and New Testaments, can be

explained by the shift from the old to the new
covenant, with the new superseding the old, as
Hebrews outlines, and as Paul summarizes in
Colossians ("These [Jewish religious festivals etc]
are a shadow of the things that were to come; the
reality, however, is found in Christ" – 2:17, my
insert). For example, e.g. who was it that used the
thirty silver coins to pay for the field the traitor
Judas died in? The chief priests (Matthew's account
in 27:1-10) or Judas? (Luke's account in Acts
1:18). This can be explained by the different angles
witnesses saw events from, the details they chose
to focus on, and the theological purpose of their
accounts or letters. Digressions were common in
ancient literature and are not to cause doubt on
the truthfulness of the differing accounts. Consider
how four different people seeing a road traffic
accident from different places will see different
things, or how editors will often edit out or
emphasize certain things throughout a document.
In the case of Judas, the simplest way to explain
the seeming contradiction is that the chief priests
took the money (which Judas had) and bought the
field with it for him – it was not to be put into the
temple treasury. In any case, it is not the central
aspect of the story, the key point is the fulfilment
of prophecy and Judas' demise.

47   Groothuis, "Equal in Being, Unequal in Role:
     Exploring the Logic of Woman's Subordination,"
     In Discovering Biblical Equality: Complementarity

Without Hierarchy, 313; Neuer, Man & Woman in Christian Perspective, 125; Bordwine, The Pauline Doctrine of Male Headship. The Apostle versus Biblical Feminists, 120; Piper, "An Overview of Critical Concerns: Questions and Answers," In Recovering Biblical Manhood and Womanhood, 56; Knight, "Husbands and Wives as Analogies of Christ and the Church: Ephesians 5:21-33 and Colossians 3:18-19," In Recovering Biblical Manhood and Womanhood, 162; Wall, Colossians and Philemon. The IVP New Testament Commentary Series, 157; O'Brien, The Letter to the Ephesians. The Pillar New Testament Commentary, 412.

48 "Heart" (kardia – Matthew 19:8), "mind" (dianonia – Matthew 22:37, phrenes – Romans 8:6, nous – Luke 24:45), "soul" (psuche – Matthew 11:29), "conscience" (suneidesis – 2 Corinthians 1:12), "inner self" (1 Peter 3:4), and "inner man" (2 Corinthians 4:16).

49 Edward Welch, Blame it on the Brain: Distinguishing Chemical Imbalances, Brain Disorders, and Disobedience (Phillipsburg: P&R Publishing, 1998), 35.

50 Leland Ryken, James Wilhoit, and Tremper Longman, ed. Dictionary of Biblical Imagery: An encyclopedic exploration of the images, symbols, motifs, metaphors, figures of speech and literary

patterns of the Bible (Downers Grove: InterVarsity Press, 1998), 368.

51   _____., 36; Howard Eyrich and William Hines, Curing the Heart: A Model for Biblical Counseling (Fearn: Christian Focus Publications Ltd., 2002), 45.

52   _____., 45; Welch, Blame it on the Brain: Distinguishing Chemical Imbalances, Brain Disorders, and Disobedience, 36.

53   George Scipione, "Worry," CCEF – West San Diego 92. CD ibc9233.

54   Grudem, Systematic Theology: An Introduction to Biblical Doctrine, 173, 174, 190, 193, 195, 197-206, 216; Berkhof: Systematic Theology, 71-73.

55   Pryde and Needham, A Biblical Perspective of What to Do When You Are Abused By Your Husband, 59.

56   Priolo, "Helping People Pleasers," National Association of Nouthetic Counselors.

57   Wayne Grudem, Systematic Theology: An Introduction to Biblical Doctrine (Leicester: Intervarsity Press, 1994), 96-97.

58 Welch, When People Are Big and God is Small, 96-97.

59 Jim Newheiser, "Anger/Abuse," Institute for Biblical Counseling & Discipleship.

60 _____.

61 _____., Wayne Mack, "Loneliness & Self-Pity#1: How to Handle Loneliness," The Dr. Wayne Mack Library. CDWM4191.

62 _____. 144.

63 Grudem, Systematic Theology: An Introduction to Biblical Doctrine, 173, 174, 190, 193, 195, 197-206, 216; Berkhof: Systematic Theology, 71-73.

64 Berkhof, Systematic Theology, 558.

Made in the USA
Middletown, DE
11 October 2023

40629920R00086